UTOPIA
fact or fiction?

THE EVIDENCE FROM
THE AMERICAS

Lorainne Stobbart

ALAN SUTTON

First published in the United Kingdom in 1992 by
Alan Sutton Publishing Ltd · Phoenix Mill · Stroud · Gloucestershire

First published in the United States of America in 1992 by
Alan Sutton Publishing Inc · Wolfeboro Falls · NH 03896-0848

British Library Cataloguing in Publication Data

Stobbart, Lorainne G.
Utopia – Fact or Fiction?
I. Title
321.07

ISBN 0–7509–0077–6

Library of Congress Cataloging in Publication Data applied for

Typeset in Garamond 12/13.
Typesetting and origination by
Alan Sutton Publishing Limited.
Printed in Great Britain by
The Bath Press Ltd, Avon.

Contents

List of Illustrations

Photographs and illustrations are reproduced by kind permission of: the Bodleian Library, Oxford (2, 3, 4); the British Library (9); The Lord St Oswald, Nostell Priory and The National Trust (1); Mexican Ministry of Tourism (7, 8).

Author's Note

Unless stated otherwise, the translations used here from texts in languages other than English have been made by me. I have not attempted to reproduce the exact wording, as in some cases this was impossible, but have adhered to what I believe were the intentions of the original author. On occasion this has meant the alteration of punctuation. Where the spelling of proper names differed I have standardized them, mainly using those most familiar to the English-reading public. Where several names are used for the same area, such as the accounts used from the region of Acalan, I have used the one employed by Scholes and Roys in their work on the same area.

Preface

The genesis of this book lies in my own hurt pride. For more than twenty years my four children and I had lived in various parts of the world with my engineer husband. Before going to any new country we would read as much as we could on the people, their history and customs. By the time we were sent to Mexico the children were old enough to allow me more free time and after a visit to the wonderful Museum of Anthropology in Mexico City I decided the time had come to start some serious study. To my despair, because I had no previous university degree, I was, quite rightly, refused admission to any of the Mexican universities to pursue further studies.

Upon our return to the UK, resolving that the same thing would never happen again, I applied to our local Teesside Polytechnic to take a history honours degree and was accepted (thanks to the faith of Dr Yelland, the admissions officer for that year). As a mature (over forty) student I alternated between elation at being allowed to study and abject fear of failure, a feeling common to many mature students. My tutors there, especially in the departments of History and History of Ideas, were superb. They comforted, consoled and encouraged me even when my spelling, punctuation and writing abilities seemed inadequate to express the ideas that came flooding in.

My first ever introduction to Thomas More and *Utopia* was through an interdisciplinary literature/history course on the Renaissance. Having read some books on Amerindian life during our travels and knowing absolutely nothing about More, literature or the previous interpretations of the book, I took at face value More's claim in his letters and text that he was writing of an actual society in the New World. I could see the similarities in some of the more obvious customs, such as the priestly feather-embroidered cloak. The only thing that puzzled me was which of the three advanced societies More was describing: the Inca, Aztec or Maya.

The edition of *Utopia* I read was a small pocket edition with no notes or commentary so I decided that the answer to my question would be found in a more comprehensive edition. As volume four of *The Yale Edition of the Complete Works of Saint Thomas More* (referred to hereafter as CW) was the biggest in our library I selected that as the one I would read. Now that my book has been accepted for publication after seven long years of suffering and learning, I can laugh at the naïvety of my emotions as I read the accepted scholarly interpretation that More's masterpiece was a work of fiction with no factual basis whatsoever. I was dumbfounded and sufficiently arrogant to think that past interpreters did not know what they were talking about.

It was at this point that the man directly responsible for this book made his appearance as guide and mentor. Dr Pollard, one of the principal history lecturers at the polytechnic did not laugh or ridicule my ideas, nor did he try to dampen my enthusiasm. Instead he set me various esays in which I was to set out my ideas and argument. From these it was only logical that the argument would be continued for my final year dissertation. My access to primary source material on the New World was limited in the north-east of England, although the library staff and tutors from every faculty did their best to help.

When the results of the dissertations were posted both Dr Pollard and my external examiner, Dieter Peetz of Nottingham University, were convinced that I could not leave the argument there and had now to go on and write a book enlarging the scope of my argument with additional material from further research in Spain. I was uncertain that I was capable of such a task but they had faith in me and so I decided to try.

Fate also played a part. My husband was asked to return to Spain on contract. This meant that I was able to make extended visits to the libraries and archives in that country. It remains a source of wonder and delight to me how the staff in such places show so much courtesy and untiring patience to inexperienced and nervous researchers. My thanks to all of them, especially in the Archivo de Indias of Seville and the British Library reading and map rooms.

During the next two years I amassed millions of words of notes and like all beginners I was convinced that every single one was invaluable. During those years and the following two, Tony Pollard continued to read and advise on the many drafts I prepared. Although he did not agree with many of my opinions and conclusions on More and his times he never tried to persuade me to modify or change them. He only insisted that I attempt to present them in a reasoned, structured way. If I have succeeded to some degree with this it is thanks to him; if I have failed or fallen down in some areas it is most probably where I have chosen to ignore his advice and the fault is mine.

At the end of this time I had what I thought was a finished, polished manuscript. It became apparent, however, that my background as a recently graduated historian in a field more properly thought of as, and more closely associated with, anthropology would not impress those I wanted to read my book. Deciding that if what was needed to improve the text and get my argument aired was a more extensive grounding in that subject area, I applied to the University of Durham to read for a Masters Degree in anthropology. To my relief and surprise I was accepted and awarded the degree. For this I have to thank the encouragement given to me by all my tutors at Durham, especially Drs C.J. Gullick and R. Layton.

Now, feeling a little more confident, I set about rewriting the entire book. At this stage Alan Sutton agreed to accept my book. The tale does not end there because, with the help of his editorial staff, I was encouraged to see my manuscript through the eyes of a critical reader and with this image before me I did my final rewrite and editing. Through all this the staff were very patient and kind, my thanks to them, especially Roger Thorp, Clare Bishop and Peter Clifford.

I would also like to acknowledge the support and encouragement I received from my fellow students, especially Audrey Morrow and Angela Rhodes; their endless cups of tea, and often something stronger, kept me going.

It is to my family, however, that I offer my greatest thanks. Like all families who have a member with a one track mind, it was they who bore the brunt of the daily grind over the years I was absorbed in study and writing.

Both male and female members coped not only with all of the swings of mood but also with most of the boring household chores. I once swore my only dedication would be 'This book was written despite my family', but have to admit that this was after they imposed a temporary ban on the words More, Maya or related subjects. I could never have achieved any of this without their support, faith and love, especially that of my husband who has been forced to read the text almost as often as I have. My thanks and love to all of you.

January, 1992   La Franca
                                                                Asturias
                                                                Spain

INTRODUCTION
The Argument

CHAPTER 1

Utopia: An Overview

Utopia: Imaginary place with perfect social and political system; ideally perfect place or state of things. mod. L. = nowhere. f. Gk *ou* – not + *topos* – place. From the book by Thomas More *Utopia*.

The above definition is an entry taken from the *Concise Oxford English Dictionary*, but it could have come from any. The words 'utopia' and 'utopian' have passed not only into the English language but also into most languages. In each case with the same implications, Utopia being an imaginary state with impractical or unattainable social or political systems.

This book is written in an attempt to show that despite more than four hundred years' acceptance of this definition many of the features of Utopian society are not only attainable in the present, but have also been attained in the past. It will be shown that at the time More was writing of Utopia a society did exist with many similar, even identical, customs and practices. Any author is influenced to a greater or lesser degree by his contemporary society. It is not claimed here that tales of the New World were the sole influence on More; a great number of contemporary issues and classical influences are also apparent. Millions of words on these issues have been written in other works and, accordingly, apart from a brief acknowledgement of a few of the main ones, this work will concentrate on possible New World sources.

The civilization that had evolved a system very similar to the Utopian was the Maya of Mexico. The parallels that emerge when these two societies are compared raise definite questions as to whether More's work was purely fictional, or whether it was based on a factual account of an actual New World people.

In the text of *Utopia* and in several later letters, More claims to have heard of Utopia from an explorer who had spent more than five years living in that country. In the past this has been seen as part of a clever literary ploy to make a fictional tale more credible. The confusion created is compounded by the inclusion of facts and characters that can be verified in independent sources along with other features and characters that have so far defied attempts to verify them.

The facts are as follows. In 1515 More was appointed as one of the ambassadors to represent the English Court in negotiations in Flanders. The main meetings took place in Bruge and during a break in the talks More paid a visit to Antwerp. While there Peter Giles, a young humanist friend of Erasmus, made himself known to More. Conjecture enters the picture with the appearance of the character Hythlodaeus. More, in the text, explains that one day after attending mass Giles approached and asked if he would like to be introduced to a traveller. More, who had observed Giles in conversation with the man, had concluded from his appearance that he was a simple sailor. Giles hastened to point out that Raphael Hythlodaeus was a gifted scholar and philosopher who had given up a position of wealth and importance to dedicate his life to discovery and exploration of the New World. It was for this reason that Giles wished to introduce him to More, Giles claiming that Hythlodaeus knew more of these lands and peoples than any man alive.

Was Hythlodaeus a real person or purely a figment of More's imagination? There has never been any genuine search for a real life model for him because it has always been assumed that he was the fictional vehicle More invented to give the story a veneer of truth. As long as the fictional label remained unchallenged such questions were purely academic. I suggest that the details of the New World society included in the text are much too accurate to put down as the author's inspired guesses or imagination. As we know that More himself did not visit the new lands then the argument is strengthened that someone very like Hythlodaeus may have existed. If this theory is correct it carries wider implications than discovering the true nature of *Utopia*; it also means that the sequence of events given in our history books for the discovery of Mexico is wrong and, perhaps more importantly, it would give us an account of a New World civilization before it was drastically disrupted by European intervention.

In the text More describes how he invited Giles and the traveller to his home to learn more about the traveller's experiences. At first the discussions dwelt on prevailing conditions in contemporary Europe, focusing mainly on England which Hythlodaeus claimed to have known. This talk forms part of Book One of *Utopia* which scholars believe was not written until after More returned to England and is hailed as a source of valuable social commentary, especially on conditions in Renaissance England. More and Giles, while appearing to defend the *status quo* of society, set up arguments for Raphael to refute in true Platonic style. In doing so, Hythlodaeus resorted frequently to New World examples where he felt that some societies had found better solutions to problems similar to those facing More and his contemporaries.

Using the argument that a wise and good man such as Hythlodaeus would serve society better if he accepted a position of power in government, subjects such as patronage, sycophancy, mis-use of power, corruption and self-enrichment were discussed. As More was to accept a position at the court of Henry VIII in 1518 it is thought that More used this debate to express both the humanist and his own personal view of the advantages and drawbacks of accepting a position at court.

The discussions ranged far and wide to include such subjects as the Church, the greed and ambition of rulers, efficacy of international treaties, land enclosure, unemployment, punishment and the legal system in general. When the traveller increasingly cited Utopian society More and Giles insisted that he tell them of it in much greater detail.

This Hythlodaeus was pleased to do as he declared his only purpose in returning from the New World was to make the conditions in Utopia known to people in Europe. The virtual monologue that follows forms Book Two of *Utopia*. This, it is thought, was written by More during the remainder of his stay in Flanders. A year was to pass before More forwarded the finished manuscript to Giles for him to check before forwarding it to the publisher.

According to Hythlodaeus's commentary the Commonwealth of Abraxa, for this was its name before being conquered by King Utopus and his forces, was founded 1,760 years before the visit of Hythlodaeus. Due to internal strife, caused by religious differences, Utopus found it quite easy to subdue the people of Abraxa. The Commonwealth, now named Utopia, occupied an island some two hundred miles broad by five hundred long. The nuclear nation consisted of fifty-four city-states. Each urban centre occupied an area of approximately two square miles surrounded by a circle of land no less than twenty miles wide. No city was built closer than twenty-four miles from its nearest neighbour.

Every city, where the geography allowed, followed a basic pattern for its layout. This plan, established by Utopus, decreed that every city would have two defence rings around it. The inner defences consisted of a wall with battlements, the outer ring was a deep, dry ditch planted with thick thorn bushes. Each city had thirteen churches, four hospitals, four large market places, and storehouses. These were divided into four equal quarters within the city. Throughout these quarters, the dwellings of the citizens were placed in long rows on either side of broad avenues. Each house contained accommodation for thirty families arranged to the left and right of the resident steward's quarters. A central dining room and kitchen served the residents. The door to the rear led to an area given over to house gardens, a feature the king took a great personal interest in. In, or near, the houses were rooms or quarters which served as nurseries for the under-fives during mealtimes, and altars for the private worship of personal or household deities.

Evenly dispersed throughout the area surrounding each city were houses for the rural, agricultural community. Each consisted of at least forty men and women under the supervision of a resident couple. Every year ten couples were sent to these country houses to spend two years on the land; the ten couples who had completed their two years were free to return to the city and take up their normal trades or occupations. The wealth and well-being of the commonwealth was based on agricultural output and the trading of surplus.

Uniformity is probably the keyword to apply to Utopian society. Apart from the basic uniformity of the city-states in layout, the same language with regional variations was spoken throughout the country. Clothing throughout the island and down through the ages showed no variation in style. Heavy work clothes consisted of skins covered over by a large cloak. Normal clothing, predominantly white linen, varied only between male and female and between the single and married wearers. Urban sprawl was not allowed and the population of each state was limited to 6,000 families. There is no way of knowing whether the rural households were included in, or in addition to, the 6,000 families. These were extended families with the eldest male counted as head of the household. Each city family averaged thirteen members over sixteen years of age, the rural households numbered forty-two. Assuming an average figure of twenty-seven members for the 6,000 families we get a figure of 162,000 for each state and a total island population of 8,748,000. This figure excludes all children under sixteen, all slaves and the population of any colonial cities outside the confines of the island proper. If at anytime the population of a city exceeded the set number the overflow was sent to make up the numbers of any other city that was short. When all cities had reached their maximum, families from every city were sent to any neighbouring lands which the Utopians considered were badly worked or neglected. Here they established new cities built to the same specifications and administered in the same fashion as the commonwealth. If for any reason the numbers in the island cities fell again the people from the colonies were brought back to make up the numbers. This had only occurred on two occasions in the recorded histories of the island when the population was hit by plague.

The Utopians saw themselves as the guardians of the earth rather than its owners. No one could own land nor could one accrue riches, as no currency system existed. Housing, food, education, health care and clothing as well as all other material needs were met by the state. Widows, orphans and the mentally and physically disabled were cared for throughout life. From birth the Utopians were taught to look upon the acquisition of such things as gold, silver and gems as foolish. To reinforce this message within the island gold was used to manufacture base and utilitarian objects like chains and chamber pots.

Despite these egalitarian principles the social structure within Utopia was hierarchical. Rulers and governors as well as priests and ambassadors were mainly drawn from an élite group called Barzanes or Ademus. (Frequently in the text we are given both the original Abraxan name as well as the new Utopian one.) Below the élite was ranked the mass of the population of artisans, tradesmen and agricultural workers. At the bottom came the slaves who also fell into distinct groups, the top group being those citizens from neighbouring countries who saw life as a Utopian slave as preferable to life in their homeland. These were treated almost the same as Utopians, except that they were expected to work harder. Next came the gangs of convicted people from other lands. Most had been sentenced to death and were either given to the Utopians or they bought them very cheaply. The harshest treatment was reserved for citizens of Utopia sentenced to slavery for crimes. In his text More/Hythlodaeus justifies slavery as the way to ensure the proper upbringing of the Utopians. Slaves were used in all labours that were thought too heavy, dirty or of a brutalizing nature. Thus slave labour was used in all hunting, slaughtering and butchering of animals. It was believed that any full citizen repeatedly exposed to such chores would eventually begin to enjoy and derive pleasure from them. Within the text there are only three grades of sentence for crimes; public ridicule, slavery and death. Anyone who rebelled at the sentence of slavery was immediately put to death.

Although the rulers were mainly drawn from the élite, any person who showed outstanding intellectual ability could be promoted to the ranks of this élite. On the other hand, those governors who abused their powers could be demoted to the ranks of artisans. The lowest rung of governors, Syphogrants, of which there were two hundred, were elected by each group of thirty families. The next level, called Tranibors, consisted of twenty elected officials. The population of each quarter of the city nominated one man, and from these the principle ruler or governor was elected. Once the governor was elected he usually ruled for life unless deposed for misrule. The Tranibors were put up for election annually but were usually re-elected if they had served well. The lower level were elected annually. Anyone found to be actively seeking votes was banned from ever holding office. Every other day, and more frequently if the need arose, the governor and the twenty Tranibors met to discuss official business, joined by two of the Syphogrants serving in rotation. Anyone found guilty of discussing official business outside of the city chambers designated for this purpose was sentenced to death; this, it was thought, was to prevent plotting or scheming against the government. Delegates from each city met annually in the capital Amaurotum for routine meetings to discuss affairs concerning the entire commonwealth, and if any serious matter arose a special session of delegates could be called.

National religious services, tied to the calendar, were held in the large city churches. Here, at the end of each month and year, the people including those from the rural settlements congregated to worship. While visiting the city the rural population collected any goods they lacked in the country. Houses in the city, under the control of their elected Syphogrant, were kept available for the country dwellers. The Utopians could not get too attached to the houses and gardens, because we are told that every ten years they had to move house. Utopus, having learned from the mistakes made in Abraxa, decreed that there should be religious toleration throughout the nation. There were only two exceptions to this law. All must acknowledge the existence of one true creator; they could call this supreme god by any name they chose but had to concede his total control of the world. The second compulsory belief was in the immortality of the soul, and that after death good was rewarded and evil punished. Anyone who did not conform to these beliefs was banned from discussing this with anyone other than the priests or intellectuals. If, after gentle discussion and debate, they failed to convince them of the error of their ways the person was banned from the commonwealth.

Private worship took many forms throughout the island, even within the same city. Some worshipped the sun, some the moon, some one of the planets and others an heroic figure from the past whom they had deified. Others were convinced that the spirits of their dead ancestors lived among them, invisible but overseeing and guiding them. Some believed that the spirits of animals were immortal. In Hythlodaeus's reputed account he explains that most of his information on these matters came from members of the élite group within the capital city. They informed him that this variety of religious practices was mainly found amongst the less educated and more superstitious members of the population. Amongst the élite, and growing fast, was the belief that there could only be one god. Utopus believed that, given time, everyone would eventualy come round to this belief, through the use of reason and not force.

The daily routine throughout Utopia was uniform. After eight hours sleep, the people worked for three hours. Within each city of 162,000 only 500 were exempt from labour. This figure included the 200 Syphogrants, people of excellent character who usually chose to work harder than any. The remaining 300 included those too old or ill to work and those elected by the people or the élite to dedicate their life to learning. Any member of the public could attend the lectures given for the élite and those who did learn for learning's sake won the admiration of all. On returning from their labours the workers would eat a light meal then rest for two hours. After the rest period all would return to work for three more hours. Six hours was the normal working day but if this produced more than the quota fixed annually by the governors the working hours were reduced. The largest meal of the day was eaten after the day's labour was done. Most people chose to eat this meal in communal dining rooms where everything was done to create a pleasant, cheerful atmosphere. Age groups were mixed in order that the young could learn from their elders as well as providing a chance to air their views. Young people served the meal prepared by the women (the heavy and dirty domestic chores were done by slaves) and the small children stood by the side of their parents and accepted food from their plates. Infants were cared for in nurseries during mealtimes.

Before the start of the meal a short story with a moral was read and during dinner stimulating intellectual debate was encouraged. The hours between supper and bed were given over to leisure pursuits such as dancing, singing and plays. For the less energetic there was quiet conversation or board games. The Utopians were very fond of their leisure and believed that any pursuit that did no harm to anyone was to be encouraged, and must be pleasing to the creator.

This was Utopia as described by More. We shall now turn to some of the features of Utopian life that have been most criticized. We have already looked at slavery. Was Utopian society a communistic totalitarian state or, as some claim, an exploited mass run by and for the benefit of the élite? A great number of books have been written on this question; all that can be done here is give some of the points that contradict both definitions while showing why the question is asked.

The governors of the Utopian states did wield fairly draconian powers. For offences such as adultery and travel without a permit they could impose sentences of slavery for a first offence and the death penalty for a repeat; they could demand total obedience of the populace in labour projects such as road building and harvesting; they could order house moves within the city and even send whole families outside the island to create new colonies. They wielded supreme power, greater even than the priests. They alone had the power to permit a change of occupation from the one you were born into and were the only ones who could grant a divorce.

The élite earned privileges from this position of power. The choicest foods were reserved for them. We are told that there were many handsome buildings, some multi-storied, and as we already know the design of the common dwellings we can presume these imposing buildings were for the use of the élite. They could travel as ambassadors and traders, some even being sent to live in luxury abroad to use up reserves of gold accumulated outside the island, but, like the ordinary citizens of Utopia, they could not own land or property, could not store up riches, nor dress in a more luxurious style than the masses. They could, however, be deposed from their position being elected officers.

One of the other criticisms frequently levelled at Utopia is that it would in modern terms be a cultural desert. A close reading of the text does not support this criticism. We have already mentioned that music, singing, dancing and plays were popular leisure-time pursuits. All intellectual aspirations were strongly encouraged as the most worthwhile of mankind's endeavours. In their religious services we are told of a cloak the priest wore. This is said to be of exquisite design embroidered with birds' feathers creating patterns that look as though they had been painted on. We also know that textile dyes were one of the Utopian exports, therefore we could presume that the well-designed clothing carried some coloured pattern on them.

Pottery we are told was of an unusual design and well made. Gemstones, while not greatly admired, were cut and polished. Frequent references are made to monument building and Utopus decreed that whereas the design and layout of each city should follow a pattern, each could decorate the buildings as they saw fit. Finally we are told that the Utopians had a great respect for their books and we should not forget that Utopian poetry was included in the first editions of the work.

Some of the features of Utopian life recorded by More would most definitely not have appealed to him personally. Priests in Utopia were allowed to marry and women were allowed to enter the priesthood. Euthanasia was practised. When someone was suffering from a painful or terminal illness the officials could suggest that they end their life. This they could do themselves through starvation or someone would perform it for them, presumably this meant killing them. According to the text this was not compulsory, in fact unsanctioned suicide was seen as shameful.

Perhaps the most amusing and thought-provoking custom amongst the Utopians was that prior to the sealing of a marriage contract both parties had to display themselves naked to their partner. This, it was said, was to ensure they were not hiding any ailment or defect that they had not disclosed. Could this be an ancient version of pre-marital bloodtesting?

Thus the life-style of the Utopians was laid down. A civilization recorded in such great detail, yet popularly considered a figment of More's imagination. Let us now turn to the people who did closely resemble the Utopians, the Maya, and consider those similarities seemingly dismissed.

CHAPTER 2

The Maya

Pre-hispanic Mexico was similar in its political divisions to modern-day Europe, being made up of a number of separate nations. Although they shared a great number of customs and traditions, each had developed a clearly recognizable individuality. Wars, conquest and trade over millennia had meant a great deal of cultural exchange. To date no theory concerning the origins of the Maya has won universal acceptance. Some believe they were an aboriginal people occupying the same lands who suddenly flourished because of the adaptation of customs from other more advanced groups such as the Olmec and Teotihuacanos. Others prefer to think that it was an invasion of some unknown group, possibly from another continent, with more advanced standards of civilization who created this sudden florescence. Whatever the reason, it can be stated that of all the civilizations that arose on the continent of America the Maya are the one hailed as having achieved the most advanced state of civilization.

Although artifacts that are classified as Maya have been dated back to a much earlier period, historians date the start of Maya civilization to what is called the Formative period between 1500 BC and AD 300, the most important stage falling between 300 BC and AD 300. The empire that was created during this period endured for more than a thousand years until invaded by successive waves of people who are believed to have come from central Mexico. Three invasions are thought to have been spread over several generations. The new empire thus created lasted until the arrival of the Spanish conquerors in 1519. By that time the Mexican invaders had become indistinguishable from the originally conquered Maya apart from their pride in claiming descent from the founders of the second empire.

At the start of the sixteenth century the Maya occupied the areas now known as the Yucatan Peninsula, Guatemala, Belize, Tabasco, Chiapas, western Honduras and El Salvador. This area was divided into three distinct zones; north, south and central. The central area which grew up along the confluence of the River Usamacinta stretched into Peten, Belize, areas of western Honduras and Guatemala, forming the core from which the original civilization grew. The great cities of Bonampak, Tikal, Palenque and Copán are in this region. It is also here that the greatest number of artifacts and features we connect with the Maya are found. These include the corbelled arch, hieroglyphic writing and the erection of monumental stones called stelae. The area contains a great number of rivers, lakes and swamps and for the most part is buried under a thick layer of jungle cover. It is still a source of admiration and surprise that such a high level of civlization was achieved in such hostile and difficult terrain. Today most of the area is totally uninhabited.

The southern area occupied the Guatemalan Highlands and parts of neighbouring El Salvador. In this highly fertile region the Quiché Maya, a colonial people, established what is recognized as the most powerful Maya group at the time of the Spanish incursion. This region, the most fertile of all Maya lands, not only provided one of the most precious products in the Americas, cacao, but also possessed the advantage of being on the crossroads of the main trade routes between Mexico, the Yucatan and mid- and south America.

The northern area occupied Yucatan, Campeche and Quintana Roo. It is said to have been the area of the least important Maya development yet by a quirk of historical fate it is the area of which we know the most. This is because it was the first area the Spanish chose to conquer and settle, and therefore it was the people and cities of this area about which most was written by the early chroniclers. It is also the rebuilt northern Maya cities such as Chichen-Itzá, Uxmal and Sayil that have now become the mecca of tourists seeking a glimpse of the past splendour of Maya civilization.

The native histories that have survived show a degree of regional variation but all tell the same story of the foundation of their nation. Their version of the events are not contradicted by archaeological dating. The histories that have survived tell not of the original foundation of the Empire but of the second Mexican/Maya Empire. They write of groups expelled from their homeland in Tula and, under the leadership of a powerful king, being led into Maya lands. The name of this leader in the various native texts gives Maya translations of the Mexican name Quetzalcoatl, the Featherserpent. In many sources the invaders are named as Toltecs (the builders) but it is now known that many other Mexican people entered the Maya territory and helped give rise to a new hybrid civilization that can be dated from the tenth century AD.

From original settlements on the west coast of the Yucatan Peninsula the invaders expanded their area of control. They introduced many features to the old Empire. Defences were built around the cities and the use of arms and armour became widespread. A new style of architecture can be dated to this period with much larger and lighter buildings. Despite an amazing degree of uniformity in the design and layout of the cities, as each region developed their own individual style of decorating the façades of their buildings, one would never confuse a building in the Highland region with one from the central or northern. The uniformity of city planning we are told was based on information contained in their books which all must carry with them when setting out to found a new city.

The new Empire followed the old in retaining the political structure of city-states which were thought to have exercised a great degree of autonomous control over their internal affairs. It is thought, however, that up to the destruction of the northern city of Mayapan in the middle of the fifteenth century there was some degree of central control. We do know that some form of centralized exchange of scientific data took place because when corrections were made to the tables of the cycle of the planet Venus the same alterations were made on stelae throughout the Maya nation.

Each city-state was administered by a range of officials applying a uniform set of laws. Though the titles of these officials varied from region to region it is thought that their duties were comparable. The ruling élite at the time of the Spanish Conquest were believed to be drawn from the descendants of the Mexican conquerors. This group, called the Almehenob, provided the governors, priests and ambassadors. The priests, though greatly respected, did not exercise greater powers than the secular rulers.

A uniform language was spoken by the Maya, though this was subject to regional variation. Dress was also uniform throughout the Empire. One of the great fears expressed in native books was that the Spanish invaders would ban the use of the traditional form of dress. It is commonly believed from the evidence of wall paintings and sculptures that there had been very little variation in this for nearly two thousand years.

It is only in the last decade or so that the agricultural skills of the Maya have been truly appreciated. Although the early Spanish records tell of vast, well-populated rural areas, these accounts were dismissed as exaggerations because the lands occupied by the Maya are classed as inhospitable or barren. Recently, however, through aerial surveys and archaeological digs, it has been discovered that around the Candeleria Basin, Quintana Roo, Belice and Peten large expanses of land were devoted to intensive farming. Water supplies were manipulated to irrigate, measures were taken to prevent soil erosion, fertilizers and judicious planting were used to give greater yields and these are only some of the methods employed to wrest higher production from an alien environment.

When the Spaniards first arrived it was realized that the Maya-occupied lands possessed no stores of gold or riches, which is anomolous when one learns that they had been established as a nation of international traders for hundreds of years before the advent of the Spaniards. Internal distribution, which took place without the exchange of money, was carried out in the city market places. International trade, on the other hand, was always conducted outside the national boundaries in free-trade ports. Many Maya city-states maintained permanent enclaves within these ports to facilitate trade. From these centres Maya trading vessels set out to trade with nations as far away as Colombia on the northern coast of South America.

Their intellectual achievements are equally astounding, especially in astronomy and mathematics. It has only been realized recently that many of the buildings in the great cities were purposely aligned with astronomical bodies. The astronomical tables that have survived in the native books called codices, could only have been drawn up after hundreds, if not thousands, of years of observation. In mathematics, using a vegisimal system and the zero, the Maya scholars could calculate dates millions of years back into the past and forward into the future.

From ancient murals on the walls of a building in Bonampak it has been deduced that the Maya had four tiers of social hierarchy. The ruler was at the top, followed by the members of the ruling élite. Below them was the mass of the population, called 'macehuales', mostly made up of craftsmen and traders. At the bottom were the agricultural workers and slaves. Slaves were recruited from prisoners of war, through trading and from citizens sentenced to slavery for crimes.

The number of deities and idols worshipped by the Maya was so varied and complex that work is still going on to list and identify them. Although they had large places of public worship many homes had private shrines for the worship of personal idols. The Maya people are noted even today for the depth of their religious feeling, a feature also noted by the earliest Spanish clerics who regretted that the same devotion was not shown for the new religion, Christianity.

Because the Amerindian nature could not be changed to adopt the European mentality of amassing goods surplus to their needs, serious debates and discussions were held in the early days of conquest to decide whether they could truly be classed as human beings. European doubts were intensified when it was realized that the native attitude extended to that most precious commodity (to European minds) gold. Maya reverence was saved for the earth and the bounty created and owned by the 'Supreme Lord of all Creation'. The Maya had been bred with such respect and love for the earth and its creatures that special prayers of forgiveness were said before tilling the land or killing an animal. The only justifiable reason for either was – 'I had need'.

Maya dwellings were occupied by extended family groups under the supervision of the eldest male. The elders in the community were shown great respect by everyone, including members of the ruling élite. The land was worked communally and it is estimated that at sometime in every citizen's life they would have been involved in agriculture or trade. From their earliest years Maya children were expected to contribute in the work of their parents and family. Although the children were greatly loved they were very strictly disciplined. Even today anthropologists have noted that Maya children entering a room will adopt a subservient pose and remain silent until addressed.

Bishop Landa, one of the most valuable early sources on Maya society, remarked with disapproval that the people used any excuse for communal feasts and revelry. To him, and to most of the Europeans, the native people showed too great a fondness for leisure. One of the leisure pursuits that he could not comprehend was why anyone would choose to pursue learning by attending lectures when such knowledge was of no use to them in their trade or occupation. This desire to learn, coupled with a keen intelligence, was shown by the speed with which they dropped their more complicated system of writing for the easier alphabet imported by the Spaniards.

The ability to adapt and adopt features of other nations thought to be of benefit to them has always been a trait of Maya life, as has the rejection of things they believe harmful or distasteful. It is believed that the original system of glyph writing was one such adoption which they went on to improve. So too was the very complicated calendar which ruled all life, including the major religious services. The meticulous study and preoccupation with time shown by the Maya was tied to their cosmic view of the creation and destruction of recurring cycles of civilization. They believed that the same events would be repeated at regular intervals. Thus if meticulous attention was paid over very long periods of time to every major event, good and bad, their scientists could predict the pattern of future events.

Until we can decipher the glyph writing on walls and monuments we are totally dependent on the archaeologists for any new information on the Maya. It is an exciting prospect that if or when we do, we may have the answer to who this amazing people were and where they came from. For the purpose of this work this need not concern us. In the comparisons to follow we will be looking at how the Maya were living and thinking in the years immediately before the Spanish entered their country.

CHAPTER 3

Past Interpretations of *Utopia*

Utopia becomes intelligible and delightful as soon as we take it for what it is – a holiday work, a revel of debate, paradox comedy and (above all) of invention.

C.S. Lewis

Shortly after Christopher Columbus returned from his first voyage of discovery to the Americas accounts of the 'noble savages' to be found there started circulating throughout Europe. These accounts written by philosophers, humanists and romantics sought to project an image of idyllic societies living in harmony with each other and their surroundings. Many writers over-reacted to these reports in response to what they saw as the corruption and decadence of European contemporary society.

With few exceptions most scholars classify Thomas More's *Utopia* as one of these latter works. It is generally accepted that, inspired by tales of noble savages, More, with great inventive genius, projected them into his ideal society. Opinion may vary on whether the author intended the work to be taken seriously or wrote it purely to amuse his fellow humanists. Irrespective of the differing opinions on More's intentions all agree that although inspired by tales from the New World, *Utopia* is a work of fiction with no factual base.

To date millions of words have been written on *Utopia*. This makes it all the more amazing that amongst these works not one serious in-depth study is known which seeks a possible

New World source for the customs and features described. There are naturally a great number of reasons to explain this omission, not least of these the conflict of dates. We will return to the problem of dating, but first let us consider some of the reasons why scholars were, and are, convinced that the book is a work of pure fiction.

It has been argued that More wrote the work as a response to his great friend Erasmus's *Praise of Folly*. In this work Erasmus makes folly the driving principle in society to satirize the contemporary values of Europe. More, in *Utopia*, is thought to have written in the opposite vein. He formulated a society governed by reason to show the heights of absurdity that would result; in effect *A Praise of Wisdom*.[1] If this were the case there would be no need to seek a factual basis for the work, it is an academic reply to his friend, using his own society as the base.

Many writers, like C.S. Lewis, see the book as the end result of another intellectual exercise, a sort of humanist parlour game, written purely to amuse More's fellow writers and scholars. Lewis cites the many absurd and ridiculous features included as proof of his theory, no well and wisely-run society he claims, would have such customs.[2] It must be admitted that if one looks at *Utopia* with this in mind many of the customs do appear absurd, almost farcical. Many customs in many nations, however, appear equally absurd when taken out of context or cited in isolation. Despite their apparent absurdity it will be shown that many of these features were observed and recorded factors of Amerindian life.

Classical scholars steeped in the world of ancient Greece and Rome probably form the largest group who see no need to seek a factual basis for the work. The Classics were experiencing a period of great revival amongst humanists during More's day. Because of this many believe that in writing *Utopia* More was attempting to emulate Plato and write an updated version of *The Republic* using his own society as the model. These scholars insist that without a full appreciation of the depth of influence such classical works had on More and his contemporaries, one can never arrive at a true evaluation of the work. This is in all probability very true, but many of the features of pre-hispanic Amerindian life also appear as ideals in classical works. Because we know they were available to More in one form, this should not preclude the search for additional sources and influences that may also have been available.

E. Surtz and J.H. Hexter, the editors and commentators of volume four of *The Yale Edition of the Complete Works of Saint Thomas More*, are probably the best known advocates of the classical scholar's view cited above. In that edition of *Utopia*, after a meticulous, detailed study of the author, his associates, environment and influences, it is concluded that almost without exception every feature included in the work can be traced to the Old World. Classical influences are seen as the most predominant factor. Indeed if one were to remove these references from this tome one would be left with a very slim volume. This absence of possible New World sources is curious when one considers that both authors acknowledge More's great interest in and fascination with the discoveries being made in the new lands.[3] Mention of these would not fill a half page in Volume Four.

Many other authors writing on More and his times also state that, by showing such interest in the new lands, More was far ahead of his times and his fellow scholars in his appreciation of the implications of such discoveries. This supposed 'fact' has become accepted as such basically through repetition. The only concrete evidence for such an interest is the means used in the text of *Utopia* to introduce the 'fictional' character Raphael Hythlodaeus. Giles, when telling More of the traveller, says:

> There is no mortal alive today who can give you such an account of unknown peoples and lands, *a subject about which you are always most greedy to hear.*[4] [My italics]

From this it would appear that *Utopia* is itself the evidence and almost sole proof that More did have a strong interest in the new lands being discovered.

There is one reference to a classical work not cited by either Surtz or Hexter that could have had a dramatic influence on past interpretations of the work. This is the story of the capture of Ulysses by the one-eyed giant, Cyclops. More orignally titled his work 'Nusquama', but this title was dropped in favour of 'Utopia', provided by Erasmus.[5] Both titles were invented to convey the same message; the island is nowhere, it does not exist.[6] If we recall the story of the Cyclops we will remember that, in order to escape, Ulysses, using a play of words on his name, manages to convince the giant that his name is 'no one'. When the giant's neighbours asked who had injured him he replied 'no one'.[7] Has Thomas More played the same trick on us? Have we failed to seek the island because we are told at the outset that it doesn't exist?

This kind of jest was perfectly in keeping with what we know of More's character. It was this love of ironic humour that most probably gives rise to the belief that *Utopia* was intended as a literary hoax. The first biographer of More, his son-in-law William Roper, makes no mention whatever of the work which even then was being hailed as his best. Harpsfield, writing shortly after Roper, either from information supplied by Roper or echoing current opinion, rejoices that 'the witty invention' had fooled some of the most renowned and intelligent men of the day.[8] These words imply that at the time of publication many were convinced that it did portray an actual society in the New World. Those who held this opinion in the sixteenth century cannot simply be written off as more gullible and less intelligent than modern interpreters of the work. Indeed they had one advantage denied us, they had first-hand knowledge of all the sources available to the author.

It is possible that More and his friends encouraged the theory of the work being a literary hoax circulated for their own amusement. Even More's friends and family were subjected to these little jests. Stapleton, a later biographer, writes that More:

> . . . in most serious matters tried always to be pleasant and humorous, so in the midst of jokes he kept so grave a face, and even when all those around him were laughing heartily, looked so solemn that neither his wife nor any other member of his family could tell from his countenance whether he was speaking seriously or in jest, but had to judge from the subject matter or circumstances.[9]

We should not presume to know More better than his wife and family, but like them should examine the subject matter and circumstances before passing judgement. No one would attempt to argue that classical influences are not to be found in *Utopia*. A great number of the features included by More also appear in several of the classical texts that seek to give their idea of the ideal state.[10] Perhaps those who advocate a purely classical base for the work are confusing form for substance. By choosing the form of the classical writers of Greece to present a story of one of the newest nations known to man More hoped to confuse those who:

> . . . despise as trite whatever is not packed with obsolete expressions . . . approve only of what is old.[11]

What better way to cloud the issue than to tell a true story in the guise of a reproduction of an ancient work? In more recent times *Utopia* has received the attention of scholars studying the social and political implications of Utopian society. Supporters from both extremes of the political spectrum have claimed that the implicit ideology in More's society can be seen as justification of their own brand of ideology. They credit the author with being the first of the modern writers to offer a blueprint for the total reform of society. One might have expected some of these writers to make a search for a factual basis in order to demonstrate that the reforms were workable, at least in some areas of the world. Instead they seem content to see the work as the blueprint of a man born far ahead of his time, who spelled out the reforms needed to restructure a corrupt and decaying society. Just as others have failed to produce proof of More's interest in the New World as motivation for the work, the political interpreters have failed to establish proof of More as a reformer. Many of the reforms incorporated into the work were alien to More even at the time of writing and, due to imminent religious upheaval, would soon be seen as dangerous.

CHAPTER 4

Confusion over Dating

The professionals tend to be indoctrinated along the lines of accepted opinion, and they had better be if they desire smooth careers.

Cyrus H. Gordon

Our unquestioning acceptance of the sequence of events that led up to the 'discovery and conquest' of the New World has probably been the single greatest factor in interpreting *Utopia* as a work of fiction. Thomas More wrote of his urban, politically-organized state before such nations had been discovered in the new lands. Such discoveries, we are told, did not occur until the year following the publication of *Utopia*. It will be equally difficult to get some historians to accept that our history books are wrong on the dating of the discovery of Mexico, as to persuade scholars of More that *Utopia* is not a work of pure fiction.

There are a great number of scholarly works on the market which make convincing claims that the American continent had been visited for hundreds, some say thousands, of years prior to 1492. Although these are gaining increasing acceptance in many quarters of the academic world so far this has not filtered through to the establishment level of schools and universities. If such a theory was universally accepted there would be no need here to establish that a pre-1517 knowledge of the mainland of Mexico was possible.

Perhaps this acceptance of events should be questioned when accounts available are themselves recorded as being incomplete, thus leading to the conclusion that the whole history of the New World is not known.

When Martin Fernandez de Navarrete wrote a book that is still regarded as one of the best on the early voyages of discovery, he lamented that the true, complete story could not be written because too many original documents and records were missing.[1] In 1974, nearly 150 years later, Admiral S.E. Morison wrote what is acknowledged as the best modern work on the same theme. By the latter author's own admission the sources for his book were almost identical to those available to Navarrete.

It is generally accepted that the first discovery and exploration of mainland Mexico took place in 1517[2] and that prior to this the only societies found in the New World were the unsophisticated peoples that had given rise to the noble savage stories.

Yet if one looks at a map of the areas discovered and explored between 1492 and 1515 (when *Utopia* was written) one would see that from bases in Hispaniola (now comprising modern Haiti and the Dominican Republic) and Cuba, vast stretches of coastline from Honduras in the north to present-day Argentina had been explored. Florida, and many of the islands dotting the Caribbean, had also been explored.[3] The only blanks on this map would be the western-most tip of the island of Cuba and the Yucatan Peninsula. A Yucatecan scholar, Ruz Menendez, writing on the relationship between Yucatan and Cuba, is of the opinion that the tiny stretch of water that separates Cuba from the Yucatan has since time immemorial been seen as a means of joining, not separating, the two peoples.[4] Yet we are asked to believe that Spanish explorers who had braved thousands of miles of hostile seas did not cross this 125-mile strait until twenty-five years after the discovery of Cuba.

Columbus did have contact with the Maya on his fourth and last voyage when he met a Maya trading vessel while exploring the coast of Honduras. His biographers all lament, for his sake, that he refused the Maya invitation to visit their homeland. By sailing in the opposite direction the Admiral missed his chance to go down in history as the discoverer of

Mexico. Reading the reports of these early voyages one is very aware of the hunger for gold that gripped Columbus. Once more, because of the absence of documentary evidence, we are asked to believe that Columbus passed up this opportunity to visit the lands of the first people he had seen who clearly knew how to work metal. The trading vessel was reported to have had a crucible aboard for smelting.[5]

The only way this story would make sense is to assume that these lands, only two or three days sail away, were already known to Columbus. This is not an outrageous claim to make when one reads of the secrecy and greed that surrounded the early discoveries. No extant copies exist of Columbus's original journals.[6] The ones that have come down to us were edited and corrected, some on the orders of his patron Queen Isabel. When one reads the correspondence exchanged between the queen and Columbus the desire for secrecy is very apparent.[7] It was in Columbus's best interest, as sole controller of all traffic and trade with the new lands, to keep quiet about such a rich source of trade goods, leaving him or his personally-appointed representatives as the sole contact.[8] This right, like many others, was stripped from Columbus when the true extent and wealth of the area was realized.[9]

There is further evidence that Columbus had contact with the Maya in a series of hearings instigated after his death by his family in an attempt to regain some of the rights of which he was stripped by the Spanish Court. One of the questions posed to men who had sailed with the Admiral was:

. . . did you discover a land the natives called Maya?

Amongst those who answered yes were some who declared that maps and records of the land made at the time were confiscated by Columbus. Supposedly Columbus was firmly convinced that Cuba was part of the continental mainland despite having been told by the native islanders that it was an island. The Admiral added to the confusion of later biographers by forcing his crew to sign a statement to this effect. Some of the signatories, however, added:

> . . . After many leagues sailing you come to a land of politically-organized people who know of the world.[10]

If, as these records tend to suggest, the Maya were known from before the death of Columbus in 1506, there would have been ample time for knowledge of these people to have circulated in Europe before 1515. Before turning to early documents that will confirm that Europeans did in fact know and live amongst the Maya before 1515 we will examine the possibility that More's source could have come from closer to home.

Two sources consulted open up the possibility that Thomas More could have met someone in England with a detailed knowledge of the Maya and their customs. Professor D.B. Quinn is one of the few British scholars to enter the stormy debate of who discovered the Americas. In one study of this problem he presents evidence that by the 1470s English sailors had become so familiar with the new lands that they sent out regular trading fleets.[11] The second work, by the Netherlands scholar Edzer Roukema, is a study of the names on early pre-1517 maps which he believes shows that the Yucatan Peninsula was known and explored before 1503. He concludes that these early explorers were most probably English.[12]

England by the middle of the fifteenth century had earned a reputation as a nation of traders and explorers. An English historian, writing in 1486, criticized King Edward IV for having involved himself in marine commerce like a common trader.[13] From a variety of sources we learn that many of the English involved in maritime trading were of '. . . gentle even noble birth . . . '. Wylloby, Chauncellor,[14] Thorne, Eliot,[15] Pyning and Poythurst[16] are some of the names mentioned. One of the men who accompanied More on his embassy to Flanders was named Poynings or Ponynges.[17] Given the variation in spellings in those days, could this be the same family as Pyning? Thomas More and his family had excellent contacts with the world of commerce and also with many of noble birth so we cannot totally rule out the possibility of an English source as an informant on the New World. We do know that the availability of new dyes revolutionized the English textile industry in the middle of the fifteenth century. Textile dyes were one of the most sought-after products of the new lands. Is it possible that these were brought to England from these lands before 1500?

CHAPTER 5

Early Voyages

An age will come after many years when the Ocean will loose the
chain of things and a huge land will lie revealed.

Seneca

The desire for secrecy coupled to a genuine ignorance of the
true geography of the land makes any attempt to interpret the
names on the early maps a nightmare for all but the expert.
Confusion over the names and positions of specific areas was to
endure for many decades. Early documents tell us that the area
of Yucatan was known by several names before the arrival of
the Spaniards. Peter Martyr in a letter mentions an area with
many cities close to Cuba which the natives called Paria,[1] a
name that is also used in *Utopia*.[2] Torquemada said that
Quetzalcoatl led his people to an area called 'Onohualco'.[3]
Landa gives three names for the Yucatan, 'Uluumil cutz' and
'ciuyetel ceh', which he translates as 'the land of turkeys and
deer', and Peten, which means island. According to these early
chroniclers the name Yucatan was the result of a misunder-
standing between the natives and the early explorers. When
the natives were asked what they called their country they
replied 'tectetan' (we do not understand you) and this reply
became corrupted to Yucatan.[4]

In the first three decades of Spanish occupation of the Indies
a great number of people left Europe to live there. In 1500 a
fleet left Spain carrying 1,500 settlers.[5] Groups of 400 and
500 were commonplace.[6] Between 1506 and 1512 there were
156 officially sanctioned voyages,[7] and one could probably add
a few more unofficial ones. The time taken to make the
crossing varied greatly but Columbus made one crossing in

twenty days.[8] We also know that every return voyage brought people back to Europe thus increasing those numbers in Europe having a first-hand knowledge of the lands.

The years 1517–19 saw three vital expeditions to the mainland. The second of these, in 1518, further explored the 'newly-discovered' Mexico under the command of one Juan Grijalba. In a report written of this voyage we read of wonderful stone-built cities and beautiful gardens. The report described a cultured population living in well-organized and disciplined societies and also reported what was interpreted as obvious signs of a prior knowledge of Christianity.[9] One would think that this last point would have been of great interest to the next fleet to visit there. The next fleet, however, led by Cortes, was only concerned to locate the gold-rich nation the natives told them lay to the south.[10] It would appear that, even from the limited contacts that were officially recorded, it was already known that there was no vast store of gold on Maya territory. This opinion is supported in one of the best and most famous records of the conquest ever written, that of Bernal Diaz del Castillo. When commenting on the poor quality of the gifts given to them by the Maya he wrote:

> It is said by *those who know this province* that there is nothing here of real value. . . .[11] [My italics]

Who were those who 'know this province'? No one should have been better qualified than the author to know those lands as, by his own account, he was one of the very few who sailed on all three voyages that are said to involve the initial discovery of Mexico.[12] He makes further reference to others with a prior knowledge of Mexico when he writes of Tenochtitlan (Mexico City) before he had seen it:

> the news circulating in Spain, and from others who have been in New Spain, is that Mexico [City] is a huge, populated city built on the water like Venice.[13]

Our history books state that Cortes and his forces were the first and only Europeans to set eyes on the fabulous Aztec city before they destroyed it. If that really was the case who were those people who never appear in our history books who could carry tales back to Europe?

In the account of Vespucci's voyages cited in *Utopia* we read of a group of men being left on the coast of Brazil.[14] This was not an isolated instance of men choosing to remain to explore the territory and come to know the natives. Columbus, on his first voyage to Hispaniola, left a group who were all killed.[15] Others were more fortunate. One, Juan Buenaventura, spent thirteen months amongst natives before being picked up again.[16]

Many individuals spent much longer involuntary periods with native people, usually as a result of shipwrecks. The most famous instance is well documented. In 1511 a ship set out from the settlement of Darien to sail to Hispaniola. On the way it was shipwrecked off the coast of Jamaica. Twenty survivors, without food or water, were washed up on the shore of the Yucatan Peninsula. Half their number had died and the remainder had been taken prisoner by a local chief. Two men escaped and went in different directions. One, Geronimo Aguilar, spent the next eight years in the service of a local ruler, or cacique, until rescued by Cortes in 1519. The other, Gonzalo Guerrero, chose to ignore the message sent to him by Cortes and stayed behind with his native wife and children. He was to die twenty years later fighting the Spaniards who were trying to conquer the Maya.[17] When Cortes was told of Castillians living with the natives there were said to be several, but, apart from those two, Cortes makes no further mention of others.[18]

Other sources also tell of Spaniards living amongst the Maya before 1517. In the appendix to the 1982 Porrua edition of Diego de Landa's *Relacion de las Cosas de Yucatan* there is a letter which tells of a similar event.[19] Attempts to trace the original were frustrated as the only source mentioned was an earlier edition of the same work. Acting on a suggestion of the staff at the Archives of the Indies in Seville, I started a search of the unedited documents to see if I could trace the original. I never did find the letter cited in Landa's book but found a very similar one telling of the same events. This version was found in 1885 quite by accident when the Spanish scholar, Cesario Fernandez Duro, was working in the Spanish Royal Academy on totally unrelated documents.

> News from Seville of everything brought by a caraval that arrived here from the mainland sent to my Lord Archbishop of Granada, President of the Council for The Indies.
> Two days ago a caraval of eighty tons arrived here from the new land called Huicata, six indians came with them. It is said that fifteen or twenty years ago eight Castilians from Seville, survivors of a shipwreck, came to their country. There they married and [grew] rich. It is a land with walled cities and towns like here. The first city the Spaniards stayed in, of some four or five hundred occupants, lay on the coast at the mouth of a river. Later they took up residence about a cross-bow shot from the city. There they became good friends with the natives and all worked together. In a small boat from the caraval they sailed fourteen leagues higher up and visited a city of fourteen thousand inhabitants, this they named New Seville. It is walled with towers and splendid houses and is well governed. It has everything Seville has, squares and a busy market. They say that another city, even bigger than the one they saw, has sixty thousand inhabitants, this they were told because they did not visit it . . . .[20]

There are a few differences between the letters: the Landa version was addressed to a different recipient; the new land is called Yucatan; fifty, not six, indians were brought; the ship was wrecked during a voyage of exploration; the distance between the two larger cities is given as four leagues and the Spaniards were said to have spent ten days in the largest city. (The population figure for this largest city is, however, printed as only one thousand, which is probably a misprint.) Despite these differences there can be little doubt that they are accounts of the same events. Unfortunately the letters are undated but even presuming that they arrived shortly after the 'discovery' in 1517, fifteen or twenty years earlier would put these events well before the publication of *Utopia*.

From the available records therefore it would appear that between the years 1498 and 1519 a minimum of sixteen Europeans were living with the Maya. Rumours of Christians living amongst them continued to circulate for many years after the Spanish occupation. Bishop Landa, hoping to put paid to these stories for once and all asked the opinion of his most trusted convert. He not only confirmed the stories but also added that he personally had seen bodies of men wearing crosses while demolishing a house on the west coast. Accepting the veracity of this story Landa chose to close his work thus:

> If this really was the case, it is possible that a few people from Spain did arrive here but died shortly after, for this reason no real memory of the visit has survived.[21]

A short life span is not the only reason that could explain why such prior knowledge would not be made public. Anyone seeking to control the land and govern in the sovereign's name had to establish that they were the first to discover and explore the said lands. As a great number of explorers were dispatched in the years after 1495 to discover and explore the mainland, many fierce debates arose as to who had been the first to claim the land. It can be appreciated therefore that if any explorer learned of earlier visits by other Christians it was not in their best interest to broadcast such news. There is another possible explanation. Up to 1527[22] men from many European nations joined Spanish voyages to the New World. After the Treaty of Tordesillas was drawn up in 1493–4 no ship from any other nation could sail there without the express permission of Spain or Portugal. Evidence that the respective monarchs took a keen personal interest in this point can be gleaned from a letter written by the Portuguese King demanding the return of goods taken illegally from Brazil by a Spaniard. He also demanded that the culprit, Juan de Solis, should be punished.[23] If explorers from any other European country had decided to put their knowledge from earlier voyages to use on subsequent illegal voyages they were not liable to let it be widely known.

Hythlodaeus and his companions, we are told in the text, made use of native craft to explore the region.[24] This would also have been possible as there does not seem to have been any fear of the Europeans in the earliest stages of contact.

It can be said, therefore, that up to this point in the text of *Utopia* More has not written of any event that had not already happened or was within the bounds of possibility during the years in which he was writing. Evidence of the New World would have been returning with every voyage and, in the circles in which More circulated, it was bound to be a topic of some debate.

UTOPIA–MAYA
The Evidence

CHAPTER 6

Sources Used

Mexico before the Conquest:

Their laws were evolved in conformity with natural and moral philosophy. In this land it would be easy to succumb to vice, laziness and sensual pleasure. For this reason the natives learned from experience that in order to lead a moral and virtuous life, rule must be hard and austere, with constant activity in labours beneficial to the Republic . . .

Mexico after the Conquest:

All idolatrous objects and buildings had to be destroyed, even the laws by which they governed the Republic combined idolatrous rites and ceremonies. For this reason it was necessary to tear it all down and give them a new form of government free from any taint of idolatry.

Sahagun

This chapter deals with the main sources used in comparing the Utopian and Maya societies. It could be said that the study of Maya civilization only started in the nineteenth century. In the late eighteenth century a Scottish historian, William Robertson, writing a history of the Americas could state with total conviction that any stories of stone buildings or huge cities there could be put down to the overactive imagination of the early chroniclers. In a personal communication from an informant, then resident in Mexico, Robertson had it on good authority that the natives of Mexico, past and present, always lived in mud huts.[1] Fortunately, even as Robertson was writing, others were exploring the ruins of stone-built cities on land previously occupied by the Maya.

The books published of the travels of John Stephens and Frederick Catherwood through the Maya lands probably did more to promote an interest in the people and their civilization than any other factor. Catherwood's excellent illustrations of the ruins they found gave rise to fierce debate in academic circles over the origin of the builders. This debate led to a search of the archives for all documents related to the Maya and their civilization. A great number of valuable documents were unearthed at this time, probably the most valuable of these was a report written by a priest, Diego de Landa, as a defence against charges of cruelty towards the native Maya in his care. Landa's text was not published until 1864 but the style he adopted was very similar to one of the most invaluable records we have of Mexico and her people, Sahagun's *Historia General de las cosas de Neuva Espana*. These two clerics, as well as Torquemada, drew on information supplied by native converts in an effort to portray pre- as well as post-hispanic conditions in Mexico.

The Spanish passion for recording and storing vast numbers of documents has meant that these early years of discovery and conquest are extremely well covered. The Archivo General de Indias in Seville, Spain has millions of documents related to the conquest and colonization of the Americas. Among these are reports called *Relaciones*. These were reports written for the Spanish Court by the administrators in Maya territory and include information on pre-hispanic as well as contemporary conditions.

There is a danger in placing too much reliance on these early sources, especially those that seek to present a 'noble savage' image of native life. Most of them were written after the publication of *Utopia* and as we know that both More and Erasmus were very popular there is a danger that the work could have influenced some of the reports. There is even a record of Spanish clerics trying to establish a Utopian-like co-operative on the banks of Lake Patzcuara in Central Mexico. The experiment failed, but it does make us aware that More's book was known and admired.[2]

Modern studies that rely on anthropology, ethnology and archaeology help us arrive at a more critical view and balance out some of the more obvious bias both for and against the native population.

It was stated that one of the reasons why the fleet of the voyage of 1517 was sent to the mainland was to capture people to work as slave labour on the islands of Cuba and Hispaniola.[3] By this date the indigenous population of these and the other Caribbean Islands was almost extinct. This rapid decline in the numbers of the population was also to effect Mexico after 1519. One of the most destructive elements was the introduction of European diseases. The native population had no natural immunity to these and the death toll is said to have been very high. War, cruelty and murder also took its toll and the very high death rate should be kept in mind when we read of the rapid disintegration of the native culture. The following table from a study of the population of mainland Mexico may give some idea of the extent of this devastation:

Pre- 1519	25,000,000
Pre- 1548	6,000,000
Pre- 1568	3,000,000
Pre- 1580	1,900,000[4]

Bartolome de Las Casas, writing in the sixteenth century, was accused of gross exaggeration when he estimated that between twelve and thirteen million had died since the arrival of the Spaniards.[5] Some historians even today would still agree with this opinion of Las Casas, but as our understanding of pre-hispanic conditions increases we are beginning to realize that in the past figures have always erred on the side of underestimation.

When the Spaniards arrived in Mexico it is estimated that the Maya possessed thousands of books containing a written account of their history and sciences. In an excess of religious zeal the clerics burned all but three. The longest of these, the Dresden Codex, is believed to be an eleventh-century copy of an even older work. A great deal of this has still not been deciphered. Fortunately it proved quite simple to teach the native people to write in the Maya language using our alphabet. The Maya using this system wrote out what could be remembered from their destroyed books. From this we get the many regional variations of the *Book of Chilam Balam* and the *Popul Vuh*. We can add some indigenous songs and prayers to these native books to give us some view of their histories from their own point of view.

It is not my intention here to argue that *Utopia* is nothing more than a factual account or history of the Maya. More states quite explicitly in the text that what he is seeking to demonstrate are the best features of Utopian life. Any comparisons made must therefore use only the best features of the other society. Anyone seeking a more balanced view of Maya civilization will find it in some of the books on the Maya listed in the bibliography.

The bulk of quotes from *Utopia* cited here come from volume four of *The Yale Edition of the Complete Works of Saint Thomas More*. Occasional references are made to the Robinson translation: when this occurs it is cited in the end notes. Textual comparisons can be incredibly boring to all but the most fiercely committed. For this reason and not because of any lack of material for comparison, an attempt has been made to keep these to an absolute minimum.

There are some obvious points for discussion that have not been tackled such as the mention in *Utopia* of beasts of burden. At this point no explanation is offered as to why More would include such items if he was relating a factual account of a nation where none existed. My only reply is that the weight of the other evidence is so overwhelming that such questions can afford to remain unanswered for the present, but may repay further research.

CHAPTER 7

The Island of Utopia

As the report goes and the appearance of the ground shows, the island once was not surrounded by sea.

Utopia

. . . it is thought, though as yet not verified that they can cross from here right to the other sea, making this land known as Yucatan an island.

Cortes

At first glance there would not appear to be grounds for claiming that the Yucatan Peninsula could be the island of Utopia. Both versions of the map of Utopia included in the CW edition show quite clearly a circular island totally surrounded by water with no other land close to it. An examination of the text, however, discloses that the illustrations bear no similarity to the documentary description. In fact, they are so dissimilar that one must surely question the relevance of one of the two. As the following chapters set out, evidence of other similarities between Maya society and the text of *Utopia* is so strong that it cannot easily be dismissed. Hence we are left questioning the authenticity of the map anyway. It may, however, be the case that the style of the Utopian map was copied from a traditional Maya circular map, an argument developed later (*see* Chapter 16).

In the text we read that the area concerned does not look like an island because it was created artificially:

[Utopus] . . . then ordered the excavation of fifteen miles on the side where the land was connected with the continent and caused the sea to flow around the land.[1]

Taking this into account the two areas now bear a closer resemblance. Both Utopia and Yucatan are part of a greater land mass (continent), and up until the end of the sixteenth century the belief persisted that Yucatan was an island. Many of the early maps show the area as an island. In 1518 and 1519 Grijalba and Cortes were instructed to 'explore and populate the islands of San Juan de Uloa, Pannes and Yucatan'. They were also instructed to find out if those areas really were islands or part of the mainland.[2] If Cortes came to any conclusion the findings were not made widely known because Bishop Landa, writing nearly forty years later, starts his *Relacion* with the words:

Yucatan is not an island . . . as some think, but mainland . . . .[3]

Early maps of the area show that the Candeleria and San Pedro rivers were artificialy joined and it was believed that these in turn joined the Usamacinta River to aid the transport of goods.[4] Therefore we can say that the technique of joining up rivers was known to the Maya.

Utopia is said to measure an average of 200 miles broad by a 'circumference' of 500 miles.[5] If we use today's concept of the word circumference for the island this would not fit in with the rest of the physical description we are given. You could not possibly fit the cities of Utopia into a strip 200 miles by 50 miles. If, however, we accept the 500 figure as referring to the length this would also give us the approximate dimensions of Maya-occupied territory at the start of the sixteenth century.[6] The island of Utopia has an outline that resembles a crescent moon.[7] On some of the early maps the pointed horn at the top of the Yucatan was repeated at the bottom giving it too a crescent shape. One enters the island of Utopia via a large protected bay on the shorter coast, on the sea side the bay is almost closed by a large crag which houses a fort for the protection of the island. Navigation within the bay is so hazardous because of hidden snags and rocks that navigational aids are fixed to landmarks on the shore to prevent collisions. This bay or lagoon is used by all the peoples of the island.[8]

The tides and currents around the Yucatan are some of the most treacherous in the world.[9] Natural harbours or safe anchorage are so scarce that the early explorers preferred to anchor well out to sea. One of the few places where a closer approach to the shore can be made is in the Lagoon of Terminos on the shorter west coast. The mouth of this bay is almost completely blocked by Carmen Island and Bernal Diaz del Castillo described buildings he saw on the island during his visit in 1518.[10] When the Spaniards arrived this bay was a hive of industry being ringed by a circle of free trade ports that served the whole of Mexico.[11] Despite this, sailing within the bay was extremely hazardous and, as in Utopia, the problem was solved by placing navigational aids around the shoreline.[12]

The remaining coastline of Utopia is defended by a chain of well-built fortresses. These were designed to incorporate natural defences into man-made ones so that a few defenders could ward off attacks by much larger forces.[13] Tulum, on the east coast of the Yucatan Peninsula is one of the few remaining sites of a series of watchtowers, forts and cities that ringed the coastline. The sea approach is guarded by steep cliffs and the land-locked side of the city was surrounded by walls.[14]

Hythlodaeus at this point in the narrative introduces the first of many references to Utopian history. Here we are told of King Utopus's victory over the Abraxans. After having subdued the indigenous population Utopus did not allow his forces to rest on their laurels. They, along with the Abraxans, were set to digging the ditch that would turn Utopia into an island.[15] As we mentioned earlier the native Maya histories tell an identical tale of the foundation of their Republic. Some name the leader as Quetzalcoatl, other records such as the *Popul Vuh* and *Books of Chilam Balam* call him Tepeua. This last comes from the Mexican (Nahuatl) word 'tepeuani' meaning conqueror or victor.[16] Many of the areas conquered by these forces were also named for the leaders of the expeditions.[17]

Archaeological artifacts from the occupied cities show a hybrid form of culture developed with a mixture of building styles showing that the vanquished worked alongside the victors.

There are fifty-four city-states on the island of Utopia, all identical in customs, traditions and laws. Where the geography allows all are built to a basic plan, which also stipulated that there should be a minimum distance of twenty-four miles between cities, but never a greater distance than can be covered in one day on foot.[18] The Maya also had a system of city-states but the exact number of these is not known. Maps showing population centres between the seventh and sixteenth century indicate a number anywhere from thirty to sixty. These Maya cities also show a degree of uniformity. J.E.S. Thompson, a modern expert on Maya studies, noted:

> There is an amazing uniformity in essential features from one end of the central area to the other . . . .[19]

The uniformity also extended into other spheres. J. Henderson wrote:

> A common basic belief system sustained social and political institutions everywhere. . . . Monumental art and hieroglyphic texts document some of the social and political ties that linked various centres. Similar interchanges took place in the intellectual sphere . . . .[20]

Both Landa and Torquemada when attempting to describe the cities they saw gave a generic description that only varied with the geographical layout. Torquemada added that the distance between cities was worked out with precision[21] and another source noted that no city was built further from its neighbour than the distance that could be covered in one day's walk.[22] Many of these Maya cities were joined to each other by a magnificent network of smooth level highways, some up to thirty feet wide.[23]

'For I will take good heed that there be in my book nothing false . . .' (More)
Detail from *The Family of Sir Thomas More* by Hans Holbein

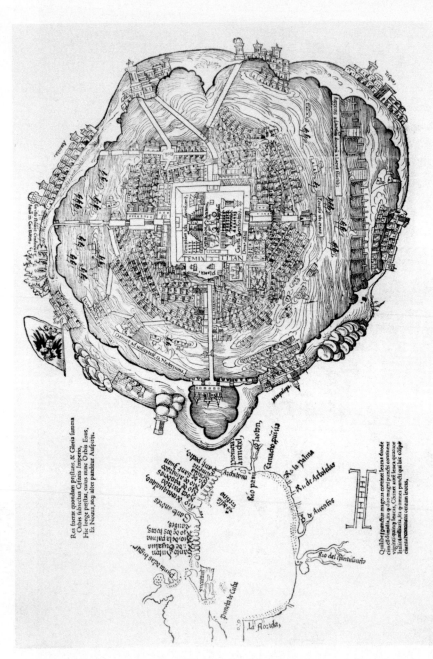

'... its style suggests the possibility either that he had a native map before him when he drew his chart or that an Indian collaborator, familiar with the Maya convention, aided him in his work' (Scholes and Roy) Map of Mexico City drawn under the supervision of Hernán Cortes

Amauroru vrbs.

Fons Anydri.

Ostium anydri

Hythlodaeus.

'Thus the whole island is like a single family or one household' (*Utopia*)
Map of the island of Utopia. The frontispiece to the 1518 edition of Thomas More's *Utopia*, woodcut by Ambrosius Holbein

VTOPIENSIVM ALPHABETVM. 22.

a b c d e f g h i k l m n o p q r s t v x y

(Utopian alphabet glyphs)

Tetrastichon vernacula Vtopiensium lingua.

Vtopos   ha   Boccas   peu   la

(Utopian glyphs)

chama   polta   chamaan

(Utopian glyphs)

Bargol   he   maglomi   baccan

(Utopian glyphs)

soma   gymno   sophaon

(Utopian glyphs)

Agrama   gymnosophon   labarembacha

(Utopian glyphs)

bodamilomin

(Utopian glyphs)

Voluala   barchin   heman   la

(Utopian glyphs)

lauoluola   dramme   pagloni.

(Utopian glyphs)

Horum versuum ad verbum hæc est sententia.
Vtopus me dux ex non insula fecit insulam
Vna ego terrarum omnium absq; philosophia
Ciuitatem philosophicam expressi mortalibus
Libéter impartio mea, nó grauatim accipio meliora.

'Their annals . . . are preserved carefully and conscientiously in writing' (*Utopia*)
The Utopian alphabet detail as depicted in the first edition of *Utopia*, 1516

'. . . previously they wrote only on parchment, bark and papyrus . . .' (*Utopia*)
Hieroglyphs, Copán (F. Catherwood)

'. . . they erect a pillar on which is inscribed the good points of the deceased' (*Utopia*)
Stone monument, Copán (F. Catherwood)

'They are most expert, however, in the courses of the stars and the movements of the celestial bodies' (*Utopia*)
Observatory, Chichen Itzá

'. . . the gallant garnishing, and the beautiful setting forth of it . . . he left to his posterity' (*Utopia*)
Sculpted façade, Chichen Itzá

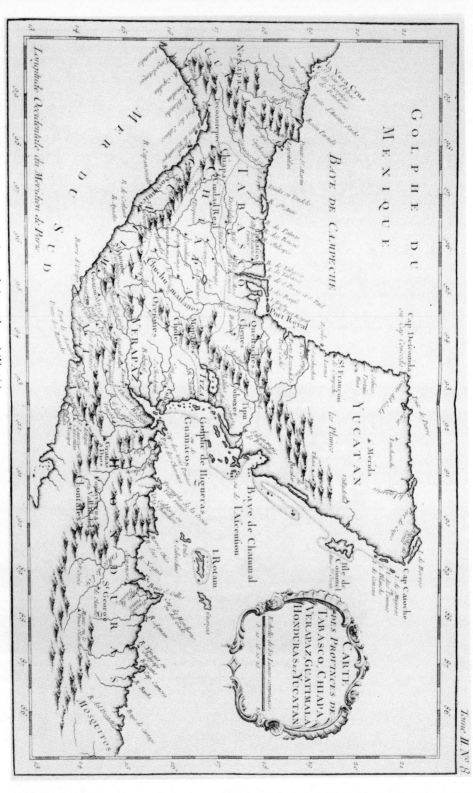

'. . . the name, which it had in old time, was afterward changed . . .' (*Utopia*)
Map of Yucatan

In 1841 John Stephens, an American explorer, made his second trip in search of Maya ruins. In a period of eight months, on foot and horseback through areas of impenetrable jungle, he and his party visited forty-four sites. Not all of these would be classified as cities but it does demonstrate that the settlements were not built great distances apart.

The Maya and Utopian attitudes towards ownership and cultivation of the land demonstrate a clear convergence of philosophy. The Utopians do not consider themselves owners of the land:

> . . . they consider themselves the tenants rather than the masters of what they hold.[24]

In the indigenous records of the Maya there is never reference to ownership of the land, rather there is the philosophy that mankind cannot own something the creator has put in their care and guardianship. A Tzotzile Maya prayer fully expresses this sentiment:

> Your bounty of the fields, the bounty of your countryside, all are yours OH LORD. My unworthy body gives you thanks OH LORD by my unworthy presence, by serving you OH LORD, thus will I seek to repay you.[25]

In Utopia the land is worked communally by groups of twenty men and women, assisted by two slaves. Thirty such groups have an official called a Phylarch to represent them.[26] Forty years after the disruption wrought by the Spanish invasion of the Yucatan, Landa could still report that the natives preferred to work in communal groups. The land was worked by groups of twenty men and the women were responsible for the hand-rearing and domestication of animals.[27] Slaves were also used in agricultural labour amongst the Maya,[28] but it has also been stated that in order to maintain the level of productivity in pre-hispanic times most of the population would need to have retained some degree of involvement in agriculture.[29]

The Maya also had an official with special responsibilities towards the rural communities and agricultural production. These Batabs as they were called lived within the city in special houses set aside for the use of the rural community visiting the city.[30]

The story included in the text of *Utopia* about the artificial hatching and rearing of birds is often cited as one of the amusing touches added by More to give a veneer of genuine knowledge of Utopian society.[31] Essays on the subject cite fifth-century works of Pliny as the possible source of More's tale.[32] It would be interesting to know if such sources also mention that birds reared in this way 'imprint' on the first person they see on hatching. More includes this detail although widespread knowledge of the habit had to await the experiments of Conrad Lorenz.[33]

The practice of artificial hatching and rearing of birds was widespread throughout the Americas for centuries before the arrival of the Europeans. Some were bred for the table but the most important purpose was to obtain a supply of brightly-coloured feathers that were used in embroidery.[34] At the court of Moctezuma it was reported that a staff of three hundred was employed full-time to care for the aviaries. Unfortunately the author of the report did not describe the method used to artificially incubate the eggs.[35]

Amongst the list of beverages drunk by the Utopians there are two that bear a striking resemblance to Maya drinks. One is prepared from honey and water, the other is liquorice.[36] The two most cited drinks of the Maya were 'balche' and 'chacua-haa'. Balche was a brew prepared with great ceremony using honey, water and the bark of a specific tree. This mildly intoxicating purgative was used during the ritual cleansing before religious ceremonies.[37] The other, although not liquorice, is identical in appearance. This black frothy drink could be served hot or cold, sweet or savoury.[38] The Spaniards became very fond of it and were soon exporting it to Europe.

We are perhaps more familiar with it in its sweet form as chocolate. Both honey and the cocoa bean were very important export goods for the Maya.

Every month the people in the Utopian countryside came into the cities for their religious ceremonies. While there, they stocked up on goods not available in the country, which were given to them free of charge.[39] The rural Maya, both in the past and today, still flock to their cities for religious ceremonies. In one *Relacion* we are told that the size of the urban churches was dictated, not by the city size, but by the numbers living in the rural areas. More than fifteen thousand could assemble for a service.[40] Miguel Rivera Dorado, in his recent study of the Maya, gives his opinion that goods were also distributed at the time of religious services.[41] The Batabs were responsible for the free distribution and delivery of goods from the central stores to the large city residences. One report states that such goods included '. . . poultry, corn, honey, fish, game, clothing or any other thing that was required . . .'.[42] The Batabs were also responsible for keeping all records of the goods stored and the lists of the names of all the rural population. Every Mexican city had its 'chultunes' or storehouses.

In Utopia all city dwellers were ordered to the country to help at harvest time.[43] The pre-hispanic Maya leaders also commanded, and received, the total obedience of the whole population. Even after the appointment of Spanish administrators the Maya still showed this total loyalty and obedience to their native leaders. Landa noticed that no one left the fields until all work was completed.[44]

CHAPTER 8

The Cities

. . . at first the houses were low . . . haphazardly made with any
wood to hand with mud plastered walls. They had thatched the
steeply sloping roofs with straw.

Utopia

The peasant houses have naturally not survived, but some of them
are immortalised in the stone façade of the 'Nunnery' at Uxmal.
The roofs represent a thatch of palm leaf, the walls of wattle and
daub. Out of such humble beginnings grew Mayan architecture.

Von Hagan

One of the main reasons for eliminating many large Maya
cities from this comparison is that very few of the great
northern cities lie on rivers, in fact there are very few rivers in
the north. Most of these centres rely solely on 'cenotes' or wells
for their water supply. Amaurotum, the Utopian capital city,
lies on the bank of a great river, the Anydrus. From the level of
the city the river runs forty miles to the sea. For thirty of these
miles the river is tidal.[1] Naturally no specific Maya city can be
cited in this comparison but from the clues given in the text of
Utopia the most probable site for such a city would be on the
western coast of the central area. In this area there is also a
'river without water' (the interpretation given for the
Anydrus). This Mexican river is called by its Castilian name
today, the Rio Seco (Dry River) but it is not known if this was
the original native name.

Maya civilization grew up along the banks of the great
Usamacinta River and the entire southern region is covered
with a network of rivers that almost intersect the Peninsula at
this level. The whole area is so low lying that prior to silting
up in the last few centuries most of the rivers would have

shown tidal flow for a great distance inland.[2] The Utopian capital, built on the side of a small hill, does not draw its water supply from the Anydrus, but from two other sources. The first is from a spring that arises on the crest of the hill above the city. From here the water is piped into some areas of the city, those the pipes do not reach draw their supply from large cisterns throughout the city.[3] There has been a great deal of archaeological research conducted at Palenque in the central area, and for this reason it is much easier to find features there to compare with the Utopian city. It should be remembered, however, that there was an amazing degree of uniformity throughout the entire central area and as more information becomes available the same comparisons could perhaps be applied to other cities. Palenque was also built on the side of a hill and they too piped water to the city from a source rising above it. In some areas they ran the pipes under the city. Like Amaurotum it too had a stone arch bridge spanning the river, as had Pusilha, another central city.[4] The Maya histories tell that on the march towards the Maya territory their leader, Quetzalcoatl, ordered the building of a handsome stone arched bridge to enable the forces to cross a great river.[5]

Amaurotum was surrounded by the two rings of defences described earlier.[6] Archaeological evidence supports the Maya claim that prior to the Mexican incursion fortified cities were unknown; later they were a common feature of the hybrid Maya. The *Popul Vuh* history of the foundation of the Quiché Empire describes the battlements that surrounded their newly-built cities.[7] On a march across Maya territory to Honduras Cortes described city defences of great empty ditches planted with thick thorn bushes.[8]

Literary and archaeological evidence attest to the fact that the Maya, like the Utopians, built their houses in long adjoining rows on either side of an avenue or road.[9] Torquemada thought the Maya had developed this style of building in order to accommodate very large numbers of people into a relatively small area.[10] Landa, on the other hand, thought they built in this fashion to facilitate their frequent house moves.[11] We can gauge the size of large Maya cities from data collected in the early years of Spanish occupation. Cortes noted that Itzamcanac, in the west coast area of Acalan, had nine hundred to a thousand large stone buildings, and Chacujal, which he stated was very similar to Itzamcanac, was said to be well planned and laid out with long rows of handsome stone houses well lit at night.[12] The surfaces of the broad avenues within Maya cities were often coated with a surface of plaster so well burnished it shone like silver.[13]

No Utopian ever locked their doors,[14] nor did the Maya.[15] The large doors in both nations were of a sufficiently novel design to merit full descriptions in both sources. The Utopian doors were so well designed that despite their large size they could be opened and closed at the touch of a finger.[16] Bishop Landa would also appear to have been impressed with a well-designed door. Examining some large stone slab doors he observed that despite their size he could detect no sign of hinges or catches, yet they could be opened or closed at a touch.[17] In the central area, where wood was plentiful, very large, intricately-carved wooden doors were more frequently used.

Both nations were keen and proud gardeners.[18] In the gardens, placed at the rear of the houses, they had a variety of plants for decoration, household and medicinal use.[19] In the text of *Utopia* we are given a very rare instance where a spirit of rivalry and competition between citizens is actively encouraged. The same anomaly has been observed amongst the Maya. In a modern study of the Maya, Ralph Roys believes that the private house gardens were an exception to the rule of communal ownership of land. He also thinks that before the arrival of the Spaniards these gardens were much bigger and more plentiful.[20] Bernal Diaz, on his first journeys through the lands, was captivated by the beauty of the gardens and he also noted the keen interest shown by the Maya in any new plants. He claims to have left the first citrus pips with them and on his return was delighted to see young healthy trees growing.[21]

The house moves cited earlier to demonstrate the totalitarian powers of both Utopian and Maya leaders are not explained in either source. The Utopians, More reports, '. . . every ten years (they) actually move homes by lot'.[22] The Maya references are equally enigmatic. Landa wrote that 'They frequently move the population.'[23]

In another place in the Utopian text we are also told of a quite distinct kind of house move. This is when families from many cities are sent off to establish new colonies because of over-population of the city-states. These new cities must follow the pattern established for all Utopian cities.[24] The Maya also administered and established colonial cities on the same lines as the 'home' ones. In order to ensure that the guidelines were adhered to any group leaving had to take their books with them.[25] Once more, the parallels between Utopian and Maya tradition run on identical lines. In Utopia it is said that their founder King Utopus laid down these guidelines. Amongst the Maya they were written in their books and inscribed in stone from the earliest days of the founding of the Empire. Where both showed variation was in how they decorated these buildings and cities once they were established.

In the text of *Utopia* we learn that the history of the commonwealth dates back to 'the first' conquest of the land. This emphasis on the first has a great deal of significance when related to Maya history. Elsewhere in the text we learn that Utopia has never been invaded or conquered since the days of Utopus, therefore this 'first' invasion must refer to one that pre-dates the conquest of Utopus.[26] This first invasion we know occurred 1,760 years before Hythlodaeus' stay amongst them.[27] If we take an approximate date of 1500 for the date of the narrator's stay we get a date of 260 BC for the foundation of the State. When we compare this date with the Maya histories and archaeological research we find that the earliest dated stele yet found is one discovered by John Graham, at Abaj Takalik.[28] This shows a date of either 235 BC or 215 BC (which coincides with the dates historians have designated as the late formative period of the Maya Classic Civilization (300 BC to AD 300). By the date inscribed on the Abaj Takalik stele the Maya calender, glyph writing system and Maya city organization had already been established. We do know that a definite date was also given to the foundation of the Maya Empire, we just don't know what it was. At the very least we can say that at the same period in history both Maya and Utopian civilizations were undergoing a period both thought worthy of recording.

King Utopus introduced a new style of architecture into Utopia. By incorporating inner supports of timber the Utopians were able to build much larger and lighter buildings than the Abraxan builders.[29] One of the crucial factors taken into account when dating the arrival of the Toltecs from Tula is the change in building styles. They too introduced the use of inner wooden beams with the same result. Unfortunately these new designs have not proved as durable as the earlier Maya designs of heavy, all-stone buildings. When the wood rotted the roofs collapsed, with the result that some of the much earlier examples of Maya architecture have outlived the new innovative style of the Toltecs.[30]

In the examples of Utopian building materials they list the use of brick.[31] Brick, as a Maya building material, was exclusively used on the west coast. Other areas had a plentiful supply of stone for building. Both nations made extensive use of the easily obtained supply of plaster to coat their buildings and roofs.[32]

The beauty and splendour of the Maya cities and buildings that were standing created a profound impression on the early Europeans. We are once more indebted to Bishop Landa for the final words of praise on them:

> If Yucatan were to gain a reputation for the number and splendour of her beautiful buildings such as other regions of the Indies have gained from gold, silver and riches, it would be as renowned as Peru or New Spain, because in the (beauty) and number of these buildings lie the most significant discovery made to date in the Indies . . . they are awe inspiring. . . .[33]

CHAPTER 9

Political Organization

The Tranibors enter into consultation with the governor every other day and sometimes if the need arises, oftener . . . If there are any disputes between private persons . . . they settle them without loss of time . . . it is provided that nothing concerning the common wealth be ratified if it has not been discussed in the senate three days before passing the decree. . . . Therefore whatever is considered important is laid before the assembly of Syphogrants who after informing their groups of families, take counsel together and report their decision to the senate. Sometimes the matter is laid before the council of the whole island. In addition, the senate has the custom of debating nothing on the same day on which it is first proposed but of putting it off to the next meeting.

Utopia

The meeting of their session and councils are very large and conscientious . . . business is dispatched with great speed and care . . . the most serious and difficult cases . . . (are heard in general session) when the entire population of the city and provinces, along with their representatives, nobles, commoners and peasants meet. At this meeting all the cases held over from the ordinary session are heard. . . . Here sentence is passed on the guilty of petty as well as serious crime. If any merits the death sentence . . . this can only be decided with the assent of a great number of people, and nothing can be decided that day but must await the next sitting. . . .

Torquemada

[The King Paxbolonacha] summoned the leaders of the people of Chabte, the leaders of the people of Atapan and the leaders of the people of Tatzanto for he could do nothing before consulting the leaders.

Chontal Text

In this, the shortest section, we are not given a great deal of information on Utopian administration. The most important point perhaps is that the nation is governed by elected officials as outlined in the introduction.[1] The Maya, according to the reports compiled for the *Relaciones*, saw no man as their lord or master before the arrival of the Spaniards. They were also governed by an elected group led by one official the Spanish administrators designated as the 'captain'.[2]

The normal custom for the governing body was to meet daily, usually at the end of the working day. These meetings would either be held in the house of the governor or in the main square. It is thought that the Chontal Maya were distinct from other Maya groups in their lack of pomp and ceremony attached to the ruling body.[3] The exact nature of pre-hispanic administration amongst the Maya is still the subject of great debate but we do know that every area or region elected a group of officials. The actual titles of these officers varied from region to region but it is believed that the duties they performed were identical throughout the Republic. In Acalan, 'Batabs' or 'ah cuch cab' were the officers with special responsibilities for the rural community and agricultural output. 'Nucabs' or 'nuc uinicob' represented the four quarters of the city. In most areas of Maya occupation the title of 'Ahau' was reserved for the principal lay or religious leader; amongst the Chontal, however, this title was bestowed on the ruler and all his deputies. The lesser officials were known as 'nucbe uinicob'.[4] In the *Popul Vuh* it is noted that, like the Utopians, the Quiché were governed by some officials who served two at a time in strict rotation.[5]

We know from the histories of the Acalan area that even after the arrival of the Spaniards the native masses still had the power to depose a ruler they felt had not served them well. After the visit paid by Cortes the people were said to be unhappy with their leader Paxbolonacha's conduct towards the Spaniards. He was deposed and his son put in his place. Assemblies of the entire population of the province were also known in the Acalan area. Such an assembly was called in 1550 to discuss the suggestion of their dying ruler that they should convert 'en masse' to the new religion, Christianity. As such a change was seen as inevitable it was decided at the meeting to summon some of the Christian Fathers to instruct them in the new faith preparatory to conversion.[6]

It will have been noticed no doubt that both in *Utopia*[7] and amongst the Maya, titles are frequently given in two languages. In Utopia we are told that these are old and new names for the same word. The Mexican invasion created the same pattern in the new Maya Empire. Thompson discussing this phenomena writes:

> That these [ideas] were foreign is demonstrated by the fact that the Mexican terms for some of them were adopted by the Maya, presumably because the Maya lacked words for such concepts foreign to their culture. These borrowed words throw light on the new social organisation introduced under the inspiration from Tula. . . . Now it is obvious that the Maya had rulers long before the Mexican transformation but, in view of the other terms introduced, we are justified in assuming that the change in rulership was sufficiently marked to necessitate a new word to describe it.[8]

This dual terminology was most marked on the west coast, especially in the areas of the free trade ports. Very few of the original Maya names for places or geographic sites have come down to us, most of the ones used today are the Nahuatl (Mexican) names.[9] The name Chontal for the group of Maya who occupied the western coast is Mexican for 'foreigners'. Other Maya called them 'putun', another Nahuatl word for 'peaceful'.[10] Scholes and Roys commenting on this phenomena wrote:

> It is difficult to believe that among themselves the western Chontal did not employ their own place names at the time of the conquest. . . .[11]

The use of this dual terminology in countries that boast of a uniform language throughout the nation is rare enough, but when we find it introduced into a supposed fictional nation as is applied in *Utopia* we are stretching the law of coincidence a bit far.

CHAPTER 10

Social Customs

As for clothes, these are one and the same pattern throughout the island and down the centuries . . . since linen cloth is made with less labour, it is more used. In linen cloth only whiteness . . . is considered.

Utopia

. . . this clothing is skillfully spun and woven as the finest 'Holand' and white as paper or snow, it is such that having worn it once you will never return to another.

Torquemada

Your clothing will change . . . they will change the white colour of your clothing, these accursed bearded foreigners.

Chilam Balam

Many interpreters of *Utopia*, especially those seeking to prove a political point, present it as a classless society. The difficulty in trying to analyse Utopian society lies in our own inability to realize that we cannot apply the criteria we have created for analysing forms of political control to a totally different concept of government. Within the text there are concepts that contradict the application of facile definitions such as classless or totalitarian.

Although ranking within Utopia is mainly decided by birth, a system of meritocracy operates as well. People who fail to perform their designated task to a required standard are demoted to the ranks of artisan and those in the lower ranks who show ability can be promoted to the ranks of the élite. The ruling élite, called Barzanes or Ademus, supply the governors, rulers, priests and ambassadors. The largest majority of the population are classed as artisans, and even here birth usually decides the role one will have in life. This is not immutable, however. If a person has a desire or affinity for another craft, if the state can afford to do without their present output, then with official and parental permission they can be apprenticed to the other.

One other area where Utopian social structure defies easy definition is the rule that all but a tiny majority must actively participate in the day-to-day running of the state. There are no idle rich or poor in Utopia. The only people exempt from actual labour are those too old, sick or young to work. Those of the élite who are exempt from labour attend compulsory classes that doubtless will be of benefit to the community at large.[1]

As Maya social structure closely parallels Utopian it will come as no surprise to learn that the same controversy and debate has arisen in attempts to define it. The structure has been well documented but the interaction and relationship between groups is still a mystery. Consensus amongst academics at present seems to lean heavily towards the view of Maya rule as autocratic exploitation of the masses, but the documentary evidence from the earliest records does not entirely support this interpretation. The Maya Almehenob, ruling élite, were believed to be the descendants of the conquering Mexicans who had ruled for at least six hundred years. Among the Maya, as in Utopia, entry to this élite group was mainly decided by birth, but here also the élite had to face stringent tests and regular evaluation to ensure that the appropriate duties were being carried out to the set standards. Failure meant demotion.[2] Equally the Maya also had promotion to the ranks of the élite. One of their objections was that at times of crisis, such as famine or widespread disease, all promotion was frozen until conditions stabilized.[3]

The Macehual, commoners, formed the largest percentage of the population but their load was lightened by the use of slave labour at the lowest rung of Maya society.[4] Among the rulers known at the time of the Spanish conquest it was noted that many, like Paxbolonacha of Acalan, were elected to office because of their skill as traders.[5] Thus even at the highest level rulers were active participants in their society. From earliest childhood all were instructed in tasks that contributed to the welfare of the entire community.[6]

Learning and intellectual pursuit were thought to be the most pure and high aspiration of mankind in Utopia, though anyone who did not choose to pursue it beyond the elementary level was not derided. Instead, those who chose to continue their education on a voluntary basis earned the respect of all.[7] A thirst for all branches of learning and knowledge has always been apparent in the Maya people. The speed and skill displayed by them in adopting and learning new trades and skills amazed their Spanish conquerors. In Bishop Landa's day the Maya showed the same respect towards those who chose to give up their leisure time to learning as did the Utopian.[8]

The similarity in dress between Utopia and the Maya outlined in the chapter heading was not confined to colour alone. We are told that the mainly white clothing of the Utopians was well designed and made, pure white was reserved for religious services. It cannot be seen as uniform in the sense employed when we think of the Chinese all-purpose garment. Males and females did not dress the same, and work and day clothes differed.[9]

Although the quote cited from the *Book of Chilam Balam* also speaks of white clothing[10] we know that it was not all white. Trims and borders of brilliantly-executed embroidery, common in the past, can still be seen today in the clothing worn by many Maya, though the predominant colour is still white.

In the *Relaciones* we read that the traditional clothing worn for heavy labour consisted of skins, a cloak and sandals.[11] The Maya also differentiated between the clothing worn by single and married members of society.[12]

The Utopian day was divided into specifically-designated sections, normally eight hours were given to sleep, six to work and the remainder to eating and leisure. Board games were popular and these were said to be similar to chess.[13] Landa also wrote that the Maya had names for specific periods of the day and night which they used to plan their day.[14] Throughout

Mexico board games were very popular; one called 'patolli' was likened to the games of military strategy familiar to the Europeans.[15] Peter Martyr, after seeing a piece of native material that reproduced a perfect chess board was convinced that the game was known to them.[16]

Once a Utopian city had reached the pre-set limits for building, a new house or building became a very rare occurrence, mainly because, as we have said, the number of the population was strictly controlled and the existing buildings were well maintained.[17] It is very tempting to use this Utopian explanation to solve a Maya enigma that has long puzzled scholars. However, only the facts will be presented and others better qualified will be left to judge whether the Utopian explanation could be applied to the Maya mystery. In many Maya cities for some unknown reason all further construction ceased. This occurred at different dates in different cities. Thompson writing on this comments:

> One by one, activities at various cities ceased; no more stelae were erected, no more temples or palaces were built.[18]

To date a great number of theories have been proposed to explain this phenomenum, but many scholars feel like Thompson that the true explanation will never be known.

CHAPTER 11

Population Control

> . . . there is no underlying fear that anyone will demand more
> than he needs. Why should there be any suspicion that someone
> may demand an excessive amount when he is certain of never being
> in want?
>
> *Utopia*

> . . . their voluntary poverty, is and was so much a part of their
> nature that they had no desire . . . to acquire more than they
> required to answer their needs and lifestyle, and only that without
> seeking more . . . knowing that peace and harmony in life lies in
> not asking for more when little will suffice.
>
> Torquemada

The Utopian colonial policies have already been briefly
mentioned, here we will look at them in more detail. Each
city was allowed a population of 6,000 families with a
minimum of ten and maximum of sixteen members over the
age of sixteen. If or when the numbers exceeded this limit
some families were sent to make up the number of any city
below the limit of 6,000. When all fifty-four cities had their
full complement of citizens, families from all the cities were
selected to leave the island and form a new city. The areas
chosen for the foundation of these colonial cities were in
neighbouring states the Utopians thought were not being
managed properly. The ideal was that the natives already
occupying these areas would accept the newcomers and work
together in harmony to improve their lands, and therefore
the quality of their life. If, however, they did not accept the
presence of the Utopians peacefully the islanders felt fully
justified in waging war to establish their colony. If at any
time the population of the island cities fell below the
acceptable limit these colonial citizens were called back to

re-populate the denuded cities. This had happened twice in recorded Utopian history, due to plague.[1]

It is very difficult to work out exact figures for the population of Utopia as it is not known exactly how many rural families there were and if they were included in the 6,000 families allowed for each city. One method of arriving at an average figure was given earlier. In the CW notes Surtz gives a figure of 156,000 for each city-state and 8,424,000 for the island; Hexter offers 240,000 for the city-states and 12,960,000 for the island.[2]

It would not be difficult to quote population estimates from a scholarly work on the Maya which would approximate any figure we might choose for Utopia. Estimates of the pre-hispanic Maya population vary from 1,250,000 to 13,000,000.[3] Having so many to choose from makes comparison a pointless exercise best left until more is known. The early chronicles and accounts that told of densely-populated cities and well-populated rural areas are still treated with a great deal of suspicion but as we become more knowledgeable about pre-hispanic conditions amongst the Maya, more attention is being paid to these early records.

Fray Francisco de Aguilar, writing less than fifty years after the conquest of Mexico, tells of cities of 20,000 houses being reduced in his day to less than 200, in one case to less than 20. The rural areas that had been well populated when the Spaniards arrived were by then totally devoid of people.[4] Frequent mention is made in the *Relaciones* to the decimation of the native population which greatly distressed the writers.[5] It is by giving greater credence to reports such as these that led Cook and Borah to the much higher estimates cited earlier.

The Maya also encroached on the less-developed land of their neighbouring states to establish colonial settlements. The struggles and battles endured by one such group, the Quiché Maya, is fully documented in their book of the community, the *Popul Vuh*. In this they also list the families that made up the original group of colonizers.[6] From the archaeological evidence we have learned that Maya colonial settlements expanded and contracted throughout their history.[7] We also know that some of these colonial cities were totally abandoned. The city of Tikal, in the central area, at some time during the ninth century was abandoned by up to 90 per cent of the population. Henderson writes:

> The whole of the aristocratic component of Maya civilisation had been swept away along with, in some regions, a good proportion of the peasant population that supported it.[8]

Some other cities were abandoned only to be reoccupied later,[9] and some, like Uaxactun, offer evidence of hurried evacuation as some buildings were left half-built. Disease features as the most likely explanation for these desertions but there is no evidence to show what happened to the inhabitants.[10]

Both the Utopians and the Maya followed the same basic plan in the layout of their cities. Each divided the cities into four distinct quarters or wards; within each quarter local markets were held where each produce had its own specific area.[11] The Maya storehouses for crops, called 'chultunes', were excellently designed and could preserve produce for a number of years.[12] These stocks were seen as a hedge against future disasters such as drought.[13] The Utopian officials were also responsible for ensuring a sufficient supply of produce to see the population through bad times.[14] In a study of the Aztec and Maya trade and market systems, A.M. Chapman states that Maya internal markets were used purely as distribution centres for the local population. In international trade, however, there is evidence of commercial transactions. Contrary to the practices of the Aztec who operated individual trade guilds, the Maya operated all trade from national level.[15] We are told of identical trade practices applying in Utopia.

The Utopians were far in advance of prevailing standards of cleanliness in sixteenth-century Europe. Great care was taken with both personal and civic hygiene, nothing that could cause pollution or disease was allowed inside the city limits. Tasks such as the slaughtering and butchering of animals were carried out down-river beyond the city limits.[16] The Spaniards were astounded by what they saw as an excessive preoccupation on the part of the Maya with cleanliness. The people bathed at least twice a day and took steam baths, the latter more for health reasons than hygiene. Before any religious ceremony all possible sources of dirt or pollution, even including used cooking vessels, were removed to city dumps situated on the outskirts of the city. Floors and streets were so clean that meals could have been eaten off them.[17]

The Utopians had specific names for their large houses, though unfortunately these names are not included in the text.[18]

Strangely the Maya also designated the principal buildings as 'large houses' (translated in the existing texts as 'casas grandes'). Once more if we look at the *Popul Vuh* we find that every one of the 'casas grandes' are listed and the number assigned to each family is given.[19] Individual public buildings were also given names, such as 'tecpan' for the communal meeting place.[20]

In Utopia one of the city buildings was set aside for the use of visitors and ambassadors from other nations. Travellers did not need to carry food or provisions with them on their journeys, these were provided by those they visited.[21] Throughout the whole of Mexico the same custom was observed, and continued for many years after the Spanish conquest. An official called an 'alcalde meson' was appointed to ensure that the guest house was always kept well stocked and ready for visitors.[22] The Maya as a nation have always been noted for their unfailing hospitality and courtesy towards visitors.

Both the Maya and Utopian societies operated what we today would call welfare states. In both, orphans were fostered, the old respected and cared for, the sick and less-able were provided for and begging was unknown.[23]

CHAPTER 12

Trade

When by the help of this philosophy, they explore the secrets of
nature, they appear to themselves not only to get great pleasure in
doing so but also to win the highest approbation of the Author and
Maker of nature.

Utopia

Look around, contemplate the world, watch the formation of
mountains and valleys. Study, to understand, He told them.

Popul Vuh

Culture, can only be called this for the metaphysical Amerindian,
when it unifies . . . ties the works of man to those of the
creator. . . . Culture for the Amerindian is the search for Harmony
between the disparate and multiple elements of created reality.

Vila Selma

The Utopian wishing to travel outside of his or her own region
had to seek the official permission of the governor as well as
that of the head of their household and spouse if married.[1]
Following the Spanish conquest of Yucatan the dispensation of
travel permits was seen as one of the major factors leading to
the breakdown of Maya society. The 'Ordinances' issued in
1552–3 enforced the re-introduction of these. Permission to
make short trips could be granted by the native leaders, but
longer or more distant trips could only be sanctioned by the
Spanish adminstrator. Any male traveller had also to obtain
the permission of his wife.[2]

All meetings in Utopia were held openly and every citizen
was free to participate.[3] In the 'Ordinances' mentioned, the
Spanish governors showed how nervous they were over allow-
ing the native population to continue with their normal
custom of holding nightly meetings which all attended. They

feared that the native leaders were using these meetings to pass on the 'old' beliefs and customs as well as fomenting possible opposition to Spanish rule.

In Utopia at the start of each year the officials were responsible for planning the needs of the community. At the year's end the supplies for local consumption were stored and shortages within any of the other city-states were made up through redistribution. After donating some to poorer neighbours, the remainder was traded. Trade, after agriculture, is the most frequently mentioned pursuit in Utopia.[4]

John Henderson, writing on possible Maya methods of distribution, states:

> There is no reason to suppose that economic transactions among social groups were like those of a monetary economy. It is quite conceivable that officials routinely collected the bulk of all production, food, utilitarian craft goods and luxury items alike – for redistribution. Undoubtedly farmers and craftsmen exchanged some of the surplus products directly at local or regional markets but here too, the aristocracy had a supervisory role. . . . Classic Maya economy involved a balance of market and redistributive features.[5]

We do know that the Maya moved goods from areas with a surplus to those with a deficit.[6]

The Maya were renowned as a nation of traders. The list of goods traded is almost identical to those in Utopia.

EXPORTS:

Utopian	*Maya*
grain	grain
honey	honey
wool	cloth
flax	—
wood	wooden boats, paddles
dyes	dyes
wax	wax

tallow	incense
—	pitch-pine
leather	—
—	cocoa beans
—	salt
livestock	birds

IMPORTS:

Utopian	*Maya*
gold	gold
silver	silver
all metals	all metals
slaves[7]	slaves[8]

The Utopian attitude towards gold is one of the most widely-known features of the work.[9] We do not know if the Maya made their chamber-pots from gold but we do know that they used it in the manufacture of utilitarian goods such as fish-hooks, chains, household articles and axes.[10]

Despite the official Utopian philosophy against the acquisition of luxury goods we do find that there is one thing they covet, a gemstone:

> . . . which at that period is regarded as one of the highest value in their country.[11]

We find that the majority of Mexicans shared this Utopian weakness. The Spaniards were as baffled by the native desire to own inexpensive green crystal beads as they were by their disdain for gold. The native would give anything they owned to get what they thought were 'chalchihuite', an inferior emerald. The possession of these had religious significance as well as bestowing status on the owner.[12] In a letter one writer comments on this weakness:

> For one crystal bead worth two maravedis here, they give five hundred pesos of gold, and are delighted to do so.[13]

In the text of *Utopia* Hythlodaeus says that the inhabitants
of the capital city-state are acknowledged as more refined and
polished than other Utopians.[14] Amongst the Maya they also
conceded that one particular group stood out 'as models of
elegance'. These were the Chontal who were said to be a more
refined and cultured people who scorned displays of pomp,
ostentatious dress and behaviour.[15]

Education in Utopia is provided for all children irrespective
of their intellectual ability. All lessons are given in the native
tongue, which is not only pleasant sounding but capable of
expressing abstract concepts.[16] Today a discussion on the
versatility of the Utopian language may seem pointless or
superfluous. In the early sixteenth century the discovery of
such a language would be of great significance. National
languages in Europe were still in the process of evolving and
standardizing, which is why scholars and institutions like the
Church used Latin. National languages were thought to be so
deficient that in order to express abstract or metaphysical
concepts one had to use Latin or Greek. To discover that any
other language had fully evolved to the stage of the Classical
tongues would have been remarkable.

The Maya language was also said to be musical and pleasant
to the ear and proved to be a revelation to the educated priests
and chroniclers.[17] One such, Clavigero, declared 'I can affirm
that there is no language more apt . . . to express metaphysical concepts, it [would be] difficult to find another that
contains more abstract names.'[18] The fact that such a disparate
people so widespread geographically all spoke the same
language is, according to Michael Coe, a rare occurrence in any
time or place.[19]

The subjects taught in Utopian schools included music,
dialectics, arithmetic and geometry, but the subject they
really excelled in was astronomy.[20] The Maya also taught
music, geometry and arithmetic. As for dialectics, it can only
be said that Thompson, after decades studying the Maya, was
of the opinion that the Maya would have felt perfectly at home
among a group of Classical Greek philosophers.[21] In the study

of astronomy the Maya are still a source of wonder to present-day scholars. It has been calculated that in order to achieve the degree of accuracy reached in their calculations of the cycles of heavenly bodies they must have kept records of observations for hundreds of years. Future eclipses were known even when these would not have been visible in their country. The cyclical table of Venus included in the Dresden Codex has been found to err by only 0.08 of a day in a period of 481 years.[22]

The Maya had always believed in the immortality of the soul, and that after death good is rewarded and evil punished.[23] In Utopia to believe otherwise was not just a sin, it was a crime that unless modified could lead to banishment from the nation.[24]

The Utopian philosophy that exposure to coarse living or brutal acts coarsens the individual[25] has a very modern ring in the light of current arguments on the effect of exposure to sex and violence in the media. This in turn hinges on the ancient debate as to whether the state creates the man or man the state. From the comparisons of both Maya and Utopian society there is little doubt that both had arrived at the same conclusion — that the state creates the man. The Maya had a horror of bloodshed[26] that extended to the inability to slaughter domestic animals. During a period of great famine one Spanish administrator reports his feelings of total helplessness when faced with this situation. When he insisted in killing a chicken himself to save them from starvation he wrote: '. . . (they) . . . wept as though it was their mother or father that had been slain . . .'.[27]

The *Books of Chilam Balam* contain many references to the belief that exposure to base practices had a degenerative effect on the entire population and neutralized the basic values instilled by good teaching. At the time of both the Mexican and the Spanish invasion of the Maya their real distress was not at wanton acts of cruelty and the slaughter around them, it was at the disruption to education, which they thought led to a breakdown of normal behaviour patterns and a lowering of moral standards. These philosophies were firmly entrenched long before the advent of the Mexicans, their writings show that they had strong objections to the lewd ways and coarse life-style of some of these groups of Mexican invaders. The invaders became Mayanized by adopting the customs and traditions of the 'Old Maya' until they in turn could voice the same concerns more than five hundred years later when the Europeans arrived.[28] We are only given a thumb-nail sketch of the Utopian:

> They are nimble and active of body, and stronger than you would expect from their stature. The latter, however, is not dwarfish. . . . In general they are easy-going, good tempered, ingenious and leisure loving.[29]

There is not a great deal here to go on but several points of similarity are noted. The Maya presents a fairly homogenous image described as stocky, but not really short, with strong muscular legs capable of great feats of endurance. In character they are friendly, good natured, hospitable, pacific by nature and very sympathetic to others in distress. We have already noted their love of leisure.[30]

The Utopians do not find it easy to wrest a living from the soil: 'Though they have not a very fertile soil . . . they . . . make up for the defects of the land by diligent labour'; 'The naturally barren soil is improved by art and industry.'[31] If, as some scholars claim, Thomas More used England as the base on which to place his Utopia the remarks on soil conditions would have been totally erroneous and superfluous. The same could be said if he was creating an ideal state; why impose an unnecessary hardship on an already hardworking people? Such an inclusion provides additional ammunition for the argument that the book does have a factual basis. Contemporaries of More, as well as modern historians, expressed their amazement at the agricultural skills displayed by the Maya on such poor soil:

> Yucatan has the least soil of any land I have seen because it is one living rock, with precious little topsoil, so much so that there are

very few areas where you could fit a field that does not have mounds of enormous boulders . . . it is a marvel that things are so fertile in this stoney, thin layer of soil.[32]

Modern opinion of the Maya agricultural skills are no less enthusiastic:

Pre-hispanic Mayas had the proficiency and the technology to apply intensive methods of cultivation and irrigation . . . they apparently had the skill to maintain the fertility of the soil by various techniques.[33]

Aerial photographs of the Belize and Peten regions show that in past ages an area of more than 28,000 square kilometres was given over to intensive farming.[34]

It is claimed that the Utopians live longer and are freer of disease than other nations.[35] It should be kept in mind that what we are comparing here are the ideas and thoughts relating to sixteenth-century Maya. At that time the Spanish search for the fountain of eternal youth was taken every bit as seriously as the search for gold. Many people believed that the Maya had the secret and the Maya also believed this.[36] One elderly informant put the secret of longevity amongst the Maya down to their regular purges with 'balche'.[37] At the time the report cited here was written it was claimed that one man, Joan Na, had reached 140 years of age;[38] others were reputed to have reached the age of 300 years.

Hythlodaeus reports that he and his companions were requested to teach Greek to the natives of Utopia. These lessons were compulsory for the élite but he reports that many ordinary citizens also attended and showed amazing speed in picking up the language.[39] We have already covered the incredible ability the Amerindian showed towards new learning and it is interesting to note that this also applied to foreign languages which were taught by the Spaniards. One educator warning of the dangers of high levels of instruction complained that some of his students could speak 'as elegant a Greek as Tulius'.[40]

Utopian books were traditionally made from the bark of trees, parchment and papyrus.[41] Sahagun wrote that the Mexicans had also possessed books for at least 1,000 years before the arrival of the Spaniards.[42] The Maya in particular had a great veneration for their books. Priests, the keepers of the records, were often buried with their books. When Bishop Landa ordered the burning of the Maya books he was amazed at the reactions:

> We found a great number of books written in their letters, and because they contained nothing that did not pertain to superstition and lies of the devil we burned all of them, an act that distressed them greatly and caused great anguish.[43]

Only three of the Maya books escaped because they were sent back to Europe as curiosities. Native books were made from cloth, agave fibre, parchment and tree-bark. The ones that have survived are made of bark from a species of fig tree. This fibre was beaten into long strips which were then coated with a thin layer of plaster to give a surface which could be painted on, the strips were then folded concertina style to form the book.[44]

CHAPTER 13

Slavery

Hence to great men who have done conspicuous service to their
country they set up in the market place statues to stand as a record
of noble exploits and . . . as a spur and stimulus to virtue.

Utopia

. . . stelae and altars placed before large public buildings . . .
must celebrate the exploits of local leaders, who oversaw the
construction of the elaborate public buildings . . .

J. Henderson

Slaves are mentioned frequently in the text of *Utopia*, falling
into the following categories:

1 Prisoners of wars in which the Utopians have fought
2 Condemned prisoners in neighbouring countries
3 Volunteers from other countries
4 Utopians serving sentences for crimes[1]

Generally speaking the Maya manuscripts avoid mention of
slaves and where they are mentioned, such as in the Acalan
text, they were known euphemistically as 'working people'
('meya uinicob').[2] From wall murals and sculpture as well as
the early records we do know that slaves and slavery were
important components of Maya society, although there are few
specific details available. Cortes noted that the slave quarters
were incorporated into the large houses,[3] and after a battle the
Maya presented him with a gift of young women who turned
out to be slaves. One, who was eventually to play a vital role as
interpreter to Cortes, had such a regal bearing and good
appearance they did not realize she was a slave. She had been
sold into slavery by her well-born mother in a country
adjoining Maya territory.[4] War was the single biggest source

of slaves; the next comprised nationals serving sentences for crimes. The return of a slave could be demanded in at least one area if there was proof of ill treatment.[5] Sentences of slavery were still being imposed for crime after the arrival of the Spanish administrators, but by then it was easy to escape the punishment by converting to Christianity which, under Spanish law, precluded enslavement.[6]

The inclusion of euthanasia in the Utopian text has given rise to a great deal of discussion and debate over the years. No one considers that, as devout Catholics, More or his fellow humanists were advocating this practice as an ideal solution within a perfect society. Within Utopia euthanasia was not compulsory and required official approval. If someone suffering a fatal or painful disease chose not to opt for suicide or euthanasia the person was lovingly cared for until they died. Both burial and cremation were practised in Utopia but any who committed unauthorized suicide was denied a proper burial, their body being thrown unceremoniously into a nearby swamp.[7]

Euthanasia was practised throughout the Americas.[8] Among the Chichimecs it was explained that one person's suffering was shared by the whole community and thus euthanasia was practised to free all from the pain.[9] Euthanasia is mentioned in the *Popul Vuh* and the *Books of Chilam Balam*, the four leaders who led the Quiché to the new homeland grew weary from their struggles and toil and simply gave up the fight to survive. More violent means are cited in a further example; the Itza strangled those thought too old to go on living.[10] A violent death was deemed honourable among the Maya as it guaranteed direct entry into heaven.[11] It could be considered that the Utopians also shared this view of violent death as we read '. . . it would be much more welcome to him to die a very hard death and go to God'.[12]

E. Surtz, in the CW notes, remarks that More's strongest description of the Utopian priests is when he refers to them as 'God's Interpreters'.[13] The *Books of Chilam Balam* are regional versions of the prophesies and interpretations made by one priest named Balam. Throughout the text he describes himself as: 'Ah kin, Sacerdote-del-culto solar, Chilam, Interprete', which translates as: 'He of the sun, Priest of the Solar Cult, Prophet, Interpreter'.[14]

Not only do we see that the Maya priesthood were known as interpreters but we also see that they were priests of a solar cult. In Utopia we are told that, when it comes to naming the principal god, 'All alike call him Mithras in their native language, . . .'.[15] Mithras was also associated with a solar cult.

In the books written by John Stephens we are given a fascinating insight into the (1840s) Maya attitude towards death. The funerals he describes occurred in widely-separated locations, but were all Maya. The overall pattern showed that the ceremonies, even those of children, were celebrated more like weddings than funerals, amidst an atmosphere of singing, dancing, eating and drinking. The one exception to this rule was the burial of a young woman who as a result of an unhappy marriage had simply given up and died. Her death was seen as a cause for great sorrow and despair but no one attended her burial.[16]

Utopian females wed at eighteen years old, males at twenty-two. Marriages were monogamous and the ideal was that they would last for life. Utopian officials permitted divorce realizing that this ideal could not always be attained, but the penalties for adultery were extremely harsh. A first offence brought a sentence of slavery, a second the death penalty.[17]

Marriage was one of the institutions that suffered most after the Spanish conquest. The Maya elders who were Bishop Landa's informants told him that, in past times, marriages were permitted at twenty years old; now (in Landa's days) marriages were taking place where the partners were as young as twelve and thirteen years old.[18] All Mexican nations imposed severe penalties for adultery; like Utopia, the sentences were either slavery or death.[19]

The peculiar Utopian marriage custom of displaying the partners to each other naked before the ceremony is generally construed as one of More's amusing flights of fancy.[20] However, such a custom was practised in the Americas. Both Sahagun and Marjil describe wedding ceremonies that started with the bride and groom naked. In a general description of the marriage ritual, Sahagun describes how the partners are bathed by attendants then the arms, legs and face are decorated with coloured gums and feathers. The female attendants of the bride then present her to the male attendants of the groom who then lead her to her naked partner. Standing side by side the naked couple are then ritually clothed by their respective new mothers-in-law. The ceremony ends with the bottom of the bride's gown being tied in a knot with the tail of the groom's cloak.[21]

The ceremony described by Fray Antonio Marjil took place more than one hundred years after Sahagun wrote his description but still tells of the partners appearing naked before each other. In this version the bridegroom, not the in-laws, clothes the bride.[22]

The Utopian custom of erecting commemorative statues to those who have performed great service to the state[23] is also well-documented in Maya history. The erection of stelae is said to date back to the foundation of the republic. In Bishop Landa's time some of these monuments were so old they had become weatherworn and illegible.[24] A major breakthrough was achieved in glyph decipherment by Tatiana Prouskouriakof when she discovered that monuments she was working on were dedicated to the achievements of one individual. To date we still cannot say what these achievements were but judging by the placement of the information on the monument we now know it unfolds a chronological history of the individual.[25]

The governors and rulers of Utopia are known as 'fathers' of the people. These rulers and bishops do not carry or wear impressive regalia that sets them apart from the ordinary people, instead the ruler carries a sheaf of corn, the bishop a wax taper as their sole staff of office.[26] Amongst the Maya all members of the governing élite were addressed as mother and father and irrespective of age were accorded the same respect reserved for their elders and parents.[27] Corn, or maize, is a vital part of all Amerindian life. It is seen not merely as the staff of life but as its very substance. In the creation myths incorporated into the *Popul Vuh* man was finally successfully created using maize dough.[28] In Maya statuary both rulers and gods are associated with the maize plant as the symbol of power. Among the Guatemalan Maya the reigning monarch used a flowering maize plant to hand over symbolically his power to his heir elect.[29]

Early accounts of the first meetings between the Spanish invaders and the Maya describe how, before any conversations could take place, all members of the visiting party were wafted with the smoke from an incense burner carried by the priest.[30] Candles and incense were and still are the two most important aids in the practice of Maya religious rites.

The Utopians had very few codified laws, preferring to judge each case on its own merits.[31] The destruction of the Maya books has meant that if any of their laws were codified they are lost to us. It is known that the governors were also the justices. Miguel Rivera Dorado has drawn up a list of the types of crimes noted in Maya records. These are:

1 Treason
2 Adultery
3 Rape or violation of a virgin
4 Theft
5 Arson
6 Homicide[32]

All of these crimes carried a sentence of slavery or the death penalty. In all other matters of dispute the duties of the justices were seen as an extension of the code that governed at family level, playing the role of parental mediator rather than judge.[33] Bartolome de Las Casas singled the Yucatan out from all other areas in the Americas when he wrote:

> The people [of Yucatan] stand out from all others in these Indias for their sound judgement and administration as much as for the elimination of crime and sin.[34]

The high standard of government achieved by the Utopians was so admired by other nations that they often had requests from them for Utopian administrators to go and serve a term there to teach the principles of good administration.[35] Maya influence too can be seen to have spread through various means. Henderson suggests that:

> Enclaves of Maya living away from their communities in other parts of the Maya world, and even beyond, must have been common in the Classic Period as in later times. Some were probably established quite purposely by ruling groups.[36]

Evidence of these enclaves has been discovered in many distant non-Maya nations. Some of these are known to have been established for reasons of trade, but others defy explanation. What cannot be denied is that both societies had a governmental and administrative system both admired and sought after by other nations.

CHAPTER 14

Warfare

War, as an activity fit only for beasts and yet practised by no kind
of beasts so constantly as by man, they regard with utter loathing.
Against the usage of almost all nations they count nothing so
inglorious as glory sought in war.

Utopia

The song and Dance of the Archer . . . is an example of the festive
mentality of Amerindian culture. It is a reference to the part
played by war, which should always be used in inverted commas,
because apart from exceptional cases the Amerindian culture was
not militaristic, war they used only as a means of dissuasion, not as
a military might.

Vila Selma

In other countries, battle scenes, warriors and weapons of war are
amongst the most prominent subjects of sculpture; and from the
entire absence of them here [Copan] there is reason to believe that
the people were not war-like but peaceable. . . .

Stephens

The quotations cited to head this section showing the similarity
in outlook of the Utopian and Maya attitude towards war could
be said to express an ideal which they both aimed at but didn't
always achieve because we know that both nations engaged in
war. Amongst the Maya we know that the use of the bow, arrow
and armour were introduced, along with defence walls, by the
more militaristic Mexicans. One of the defence weapons used in
Maya warfare might very well be the war machine the Utopians
kept secret for fear it would cause more amusement than
terror.[1] This was an insect bomb. A vessel filled with stinging
insects was hurled into the midst of the enemy forces creating
terror and mayhem. These were probably used in one of the
battles described by Diaz del Castillo and the resulting

panic of not being able to distinguish between arrows and insects did not amuse the Spaniards.[2] The same weapon was used by the Quiché in their war against the indigenous peoples of the Guatemalan Highlands.[3]

The Spanish forces quickly adopted the kapok-filled suits of armour worn by their enemies as it was much less cumbersome than their own. The Mexican suit gave much more freedom of movement while providing good protection[4] factors which also applied to the Utopian armour.[5]

The Utopians, while deploring war, were realistic enough to keep their citizens trained and ready for any conflict that might arise. The importance of Utopian trade is highlighted by the knowledge that if a trader from a friendly nation is harmed or has his goods taken this is sufficient cause for Utopia to declare war.[6] Similarly, trade and the unhindered access of traders was so vital to the entire Mexican economy that any infringement of their free passage was avenged at national level.[7]

A few years before the arrival of Hythlodaeus and his companions, Utopia had participated in a great war. They had allied themselves with a less powerful nation, the Neph-logetes, in a struggle against the more powerful Alaopolitans. Most of the surrounding nations had participated on one side or the other in the ensuing conflict. The Utopian allies emerged victorious and the vanquished leaders were delivered up to their less powerful victors for sentence.[8]

The Maya indigenous histories also tell of a great war that took place around AD 1450 that changed the structure of the Maya Empire. The powerful 'Cocom', who are believed to have exercised a degree of central control from the city of Mayapan, were challenged in war by the less powerful 'Tutul Xiu' of Mani. Many other groups were drawn into the conflict and the 'Tutul Xiu' emerged the victors. The victors executed all the 'Cocom' rulers, with the exception of one son who was absent on a trading mission, and expelled the people from the region after razing their city to the ground. These outcasts were one of the groups Landa wrote of who took their books with them in order to found their new city.[9]

The Utopians see no dishonour in victory gained through deceit or treachery; on the contrary, they see it as preferable to victory achieved through battle. This philosophy is favoured because it reduces the numbers of casualties and deaths.[10] William Robertson, the eighteenth-century Scottish historian, is perhaps the author to read on Amerindian war tactics. In his account he describes their warfare against the invading Spanish forces as more like modern guerilla tactics where open set battles were avoided, and lightning attacks, ambush and psychological warfare relied on instead to unsettle and terrify the enemy.[11] The histories of the Conquest of Mexico, written by Diaz del Castillo and Cortes, show the use of the same strategems.

When war is seen as inevitable the Utopians prefer to hire mercenaries to do their fighting rather than commit their own nationals.[12] In the Maya war described above the 'Cocom' are known to have hired mercenaries in their attempt to defeat the 'Tutul Xiu'. Some sources allege these to have been Mexicans from around the Tabasco region, others talk of 'mountain people' and Chichimecs being used as mercenaries.[13]

The Utopian text deploring war refers slightingly to nations that through the use of brute strength gain glory in war. These are compared to 'bears, lions, wolves etc.', who might be superior in strength but inferior in cleverness and calculation.[14] Had such an account appeared in an indigenous Maya text it would neither puzzle nor surprise analysts. The use of fierce animals such as the jaguar and eagle to depict warriors who saw supreme glory as that attained in battle is easily associated with the Aztec. The entire Aztec culture was based on a military foundation of warrior knighthood who took wild animals as their symbols.[15]

In Utopian war there is one supreme military commander. If he is killed, captured or flees the opposition leader claims the victory and all hostilities cease. Special task forces are dispatched to try and bring about the defeat of the other leader and a speedy end to the conflict. When the outcome has been decided only the enemy leaders are executed.[16]

This description of Utopian warfare tactics could also be transposed into Maya texts without changing a word. The supreme commander of the Maya was called a 'Nacom' and was elected for a period of three years. During battle the main objective of both sides was the capture or death of the 'Nacom'; anyone who achieved this was fêted and hailed as a hero for having brought an end to the conflict.[17] Cortes most probably owed his life to the native attempts to capture him alive rather than kill him. Maya women, like their Utopian counterparts,[18] also fought in wars. One woman in the wars against the Spaniards chose to die rather than be seen as a war trophy after her defeat.[19]

The Utopian reluctance to participate in war is not through cowardice as, when war proves inevitable, the Utopian warriors prove fearless, seeing death as preferable to conquest or dishonour.[20]

The long and bloody struggle to conquer the Maya is testament to their bravery. Within two years the great and mighty Aztec nation fell to the Spanish conquerors. By 1521 their capital lay in ruins and the vast Empire was subjugated by the much smaller Spanish force. In 1527 the Spaniards turned their eyes on the lands occupied by the Maya. Between this date and 1530 various attempts were made to conquer the Maya with very little result, in fact the Spaniards were forced to withdraw completely from the area. Renewed attempts between 1530 and 1535 ended with the same results. In 1537 the tide turned for the Spanish forces when they persuaded some of the local leaders around the area of Champoton to support them. By 1542 many more had been persuaded to join forces with the conquerors which brought large areas under Spanish rule.[21] Scholes and Roys are convinced that it was only through this peaceful capitulation that the Yucatecan culture and language were allowed to survive until today.[22] This was not the end of the Maya struggle nor could the conquerors claim control of the Maya. Resistance to Spanish subjugation continued in the areas of Peten and north-east Chiapas until 1691 and the last stronghold on the island of Tayasil did not fall until 1697. Many would still argue that Maya resistance has never ceased. Michael Coe has written:

> . . . the Maya are, for all their apparent docility, the toughest Indians of Mesoamerica, and the struggle against European civilisation never once halted.

Coe continues to list a series of uprisings by the Maya between 1712 and 1868 to demonstrate that even in relatively recent times the Maya saw the Mexican central government as intruding foreigners.[23]

CHAPTER 15

Religion

There are some who reverence a man conspicuous for either virtue
or glory in the past not only as a god but even as the supreme
God.

Utopia

The Indians, who occupied the city of Chichen-Itza along with the
Itza, believe that a great leader named Kukulcan, once ruled there
. . . they say he was a just man who had neither wife nor children;
they say that after his return the Mexicans hailed him as one of
their gods, Quetzalcoatl; in the Yucatan they also worshipped him
as a god, as a great Republican.

Diego de Landa

The Utopians have a variety of religious practices not only
throughout the island, but even within the confines of each
city. Among the principal ones mentioned are worship of the
sun, the moon, one of the planets, a hero from the past and one
divine god, creator of all.[1] The Maya worshipped all of these
plus many other minor deities such as guardians of specific
guilds, crafts and agricultural needs. In the Maya texts the
planet worshipped is named as Venus, which was also associated with Quetzalcoatl, the feather-serpent deity.

The Maya worship of Quetzalcoatl/Kukulcan is believed
to have been introduced to the Maya by the Mexican invaders and, as with the Utopian hero/deity, two aspects of
him are worshipped, virtue and glory. In Mexican legend
Quetzalcoatl (believed to have been based on an actual
historical character) is said to have arrived in Mexico from
across the sea. The bearded figure, dressed in white robes,
lived a very austere, virtuous life amongst them teaching
them of laws, good government and many secrets of science
and agricultural skills. When he felt that they were well

established in these new ways he left, promising to return at some later date.

In his aspect as glorious leader he was revered as the one who led the Mexicans from their homeland of Tula to establish a new nation amongst the Maya. The descendants of these victors worshipped his memory as founder of the Republic. It was said that at the time of the Spanish conquest he was revered by many of them as the supreme god.[2]

Notwithstanding the multiplicity of minor deities worshipped by the Maya, running through all their writings and prayers is the undeniable assertion that over and above all these there was one true god who had created all of the universe. The names given to this god varied from region to region and perhaps even person to person, but his supremacy and divinity over other lesser gods was never questioned.[3] The *Motul Dictionary* of Maya words published in 1929 lists the following definition:

> Humabku – the only living and true God, the greatest of the people of Yucatan, of whom there is no image because they said there was no conception of his form, since he was incorporeal.[4]

The Utopians avoided conflict in the worship of the many forms their god took by refraining from giving any specific name or characteristics to him during religious services. This allowed all to picture the creator in their own image.[5]

Studies carried out on the Maya report what is defined as a decline in the religious practices in the decades before the arrival of the Spaniards. This conclusion is mainly based on the results of archaeological digs which show that although church buildings became larger they were also fewer. These later religious buildings also lacked the artistic embellishment of much earlier buildings which depicted images of the idol to whom the building was dedicated.[6] The only evidence that these later buildings were used for religious services comes from the shards and remains of hundreds of mass-produced crude incense burners left on the site. Some of these bore images of idols known to have been worshipped as powerful deities in earlier times. Commenting on this Thompson writes:

> Religion had sunk low when the idols of the principal gods of the community could be treated in that off-hand manner.[7]

Ignoring for the moment the implications for the comparison with Utopian religious practices, it should be said that a decline in religious practices is not the only interpretation that could be drawn from the available evidence. We need look no further than the history of the Christian Church to find a similar occurrence. Many large churches around the world erected since the middle of the sixteenth century are totally devoid of the magnificent paintings, idols and decoration that were incorporated into earlier church buildings. In the future our archaeologist, left without literary evidence to explain this, could interpret it in two ways. One would be that given by Thompson for the Maya decline, the other that religious practice had evolved to a degree of sophistication where the people had no need of idols, images or personifications of their deities to unite them with their god or gods.

This interpretation fits in with the eye-witness accounts of the religious devotion and fervour exhibited by the Maya in their acts of worship during the early years of European contact. It only remains to note that the cited evidence of a religious decline amongst the Maya is very similar to the Utopian services in that there are no personifications of the gods and the sole evidence of aids to worship were the remains of candle and incense holders.

Hythlodaeus expresses his delight at the speed with which the Utopians accepted his religious beliefs once he had explained them to them. He thought this was partly because some of their beliefs closely resembled Christianity.[8] The Spaniards were also amazed to find that many of the religious beliefs of the Maya bore a close resemblance to Christianity. Many took this as evidence of prior visits by Christians. Amongst the similar features were a baptismal rite equated with rebirth,[9] confession before services,[10] fasting both in preparation for religious observance, and as a sacrifice, self mortification[11] and the inclusion of communal antiphonal prayers and songs in the services.[12] The Maya also looked upon incense and candles as vital features of worship.[13] Irrespective of whether these influences were evidence of an earlier exposure to Christian teachings, or were inspired by a desire on both sides to see these parallels, it does give the state of religious views and practices amongst the Maya at the beginning of the sixteenth century. These practices in turn bear a close resemblance to the Utopian ones.

It should also be noted that the Maya, like the Utopian, has always been extremely tolerant and willing to listen to the other point of view but seeking explanations before acceptance of new ideas or beliefs. The report of the mass meeting called in Acalan was not to vote en masse for conversion, but to summon Christian priests to explain their religion with a view to conversion.

It has already been pointed out that both nations practised both burial and cremation of the dead. In Utopia it was the custom to erect monuments to the dead over the cremation site.[14] In the report written of the 1518 visit made by Grijalba there is a description of the monuments the natives built over the ashes of their dead ancestors.[15] For many years it was thought that the pyramids in Mexico were built purely for religious rites and unlike the Egyptian pyramids were not erected as memorials to actual individuals. Recent excavations have shown, however, that some of them have been used as monuments to several generations of dead, the new being superimposed on the existing structure giving a higher pyramid every time it was built upon.[16]

The proliferation of administrators and clergy was one of the main criticisms levelled at the Church of Rome. One of the features ascribed to Utopia and thought to have had great appeal to the sixteenth-century humanists is that there were very few priests, each city having only thirteen. One person was elected from the thirteen to act in a position Hythlodaeus equates with a Christian bishop. His duties included overseeing all religious and moral matters; setting the standard of behaviour for the population at large; supervising the entrance of others to the clergy and ensuring that they maintained the expected standards. He was responsible for education within the city and for the maintenance of all records. Despite all this power the priesthood was not above secular law. Within Utopia women were also permitted to enter the priesthood and male priests could marry.[17]

Before its destruction Mayapan was said to be one of the largest cities but it was served by only twelve priests;[18] Cholula in Mexico was a place of pilgrimage for people from all parts of the country yet it is reputed to have had only ten priests.[19] The Maya priests also elected a chief from among their ranks that the early Christians associated with the office of bishop. This 'Ah Kin May' or 'Ahau Can Maia' had duties very similar to the Utopian bishop's. He was the examining officer for all applicants to official positions; he was responsible for the recording of all scientific and religious matters in their books and for the passing on of this information to the next generation.[20] No Maya priest wielded greater powers than the secular government.[21] Like their Utopian counterparts[22] the Maya priests could marry and women were also allowed to become priests.[23] In all probability the Maya female priests, like the Utopian, were drawn from the ranks of elderly women or widows. Landa, when writing of females officiating in religious services, always describes them as 'las viejas', the old women.[24]

The only kind of holy day mentioned in Utopia is related to the calendar. The first and last days of each month and year are considered holy.[25]

Any work devoted to the study of the Maya will dedicate a high percentage of it to the Maya calendar, entire books being written to explain its intricacies. For the purposes of this study we will content ourselves with the knowledge that the Maya also tied their religious observances to the passage of time. The lunar month and the solar year were times of important religious services.[26] Preparations for these followed a similar pattern to that of the Utopians. Fasting, purging, abstinence from sexual intercourse and general confession were mandatory for the Maya,[27] fasting and interfamilial confession were also part of the Utopian preparations.[28]

Though Utopian churches are large they are not light: '. . . due not to the ignorance of architecture but to the deliberate intention of the priests'.[29] The Maya priests also saw the reduction of light within their church buildings as desirable. Thompson describes how they achieved this:

> . . . they never placed columns or piers in the wall dividing an outer from an inner room, clearly because that would nullify the mystery . . . not because they lacked the intelligence to repeat on the back wall of a room the piercing they had done on the front wall, or feared the extra weight a medial wall must sustain.[30]

Private religious rites were carried out in Utopian homes.[31] Staying with Thompson on the Maya religious beliefs and practices we read:

> . . . each important residence has its own family oratory either in one room of the house or in a nearby building. There is archaeological evidence that these shrines were primarily for ancestral cults and for the worship of deities who had gained the devotion of the family.[32]

In the description of the Utopian service we are told that the people gather at the church early in the morning and on entering the church they separate, men going to the right and women to the left. The only colour apparent other than white is on a cloak worn by the priest:

> . . . of various colours, of wonderful design and shape, but not of material as costly as one would expect. They are not interwoven with gold or set with precious stones but wrought with the different feathers of birds so cleverly and artistically that no costly material could equal the value of the handiwork.

At the appearance of the Utopian priest the congregation fall to the ground in reverence and an atmosphere of spirituality permeates the smoke- and incense-filled air. After an interval the people rise to their feet and join the musicians in songs of praise, and then join the priest in prayer. After the service they eat a communal meal and pass the remainder of the day in games and military exercises.[33]

In one description of a New Year service Landa wrote that the Maya males and females also sat on opposite sides of the church[34] and another report says that in all services the congregation was divided into two groups,[35] although not specifying whether it was a separation of the sexes. It also describes the pleasant antiphonal singing. Many commentators on Maya religious attitude were struck by the atmosphere of deep spirituality engendered by them during their services.

Regarding the Maya priests Landa wrote that: '. . . the atmosphere of serenity that descended on them as they enrobed was remarkable'.[36]

These priests also wore cloaks of birds' feathers very similar to that described by More.[37] The description of the Utopian cloak is one of the very few references in the CW notes to a possible New World influence included by More.[38] The editors do not seem to be aware that the inclusion of such a garment is an anachronism. All pre-1517 reports of the New World which circulated in Europe, such as the Vespucci report mentioned in the text of *Utopia*, stated categorically that the natives observed to that date did not appear to have any organized religion nor was there any mention of similar cloaks. Descriptions of such garments did not circulate widely until after the 'official' discovery of Mexico, when writers such as Peter Martyr and the artist Durer, on seeing the feather embroidery, praised the high level of skill and artistry that had gone into their manufacture.[39] Sahagun describes patterns of owls, snakes, whirlpools and monstrous heads incorporated into the designs of the feather work.[40] More adds a further intriguing feature regarding these cloaks: 'Secret information passed on by the priests was woven into the garb worn by the priest'.[41]

The Maya priest responsible for the handing on of information from generation to generation also had secrets. The tests given to aspirants for official positions were given in a secret allegorical language called 'Zuyua'. All had to be word-perfect in their answers.[42]

At the end of religious services the Maya also spent the day in feasting and diversions such as plays and dances. Landa, describing some of these dances, says that they pantomimed war games and could continue for hours at a time.[43]

CHAPTER 16

References to Utopia in Book One of the Text

According to the Utopians their culture is so old that there were cities amongst them before there were men in Europe.[1] It is probable that had more of the Maya books survived they could have presented us with what they believed was the longest unbroken record of any civilization yet known. The records we have been able to decipher to date from wall and stelae glyphs present a 'history' that combines lists of contemporary events with those from a remote past, millions of years in some cases. Part of their cosmological belief was that in every cataclysmic end of a historical cycle some individuals survived into the next.

Archaeological evidence does not support their claim that Amerindian civilization pre-dates the rise of western culture. However, we are not dealing with historical evidence but with the beliefs of people, and the Maya were convinced of the remote antiquity of their civilization.

The Utopians are reputed to have informed Hythlodaeus that the only previous contact they had experienced with 'ultra-equinoctials' had occurred:

> . . . twelve hundred years ago, a ship wrecked on the Island of Utopia. Some Romans and Egyptians were cast on shore and remained . . .[2]

Evidence of very early visits to the Americas is being presented from a great many quarters to support those who argue against the isolationists, but rather than enter these arguments we will only look at the Maya records. If once more we take a mean date of 1500 for the dating of the visit of Hythlodaeus to Utopia this would give us a date of AD 300 for the shipwreck mentioned above. When the Spaniards arrived in Mexico at the beginning of the sixteenth century they too were told stories of visitors around the fourth or fifth century. Last century a great number of books were written putting forward theories of who these mysterious visitors were. Cultural similarities like the pyramids led many to believe that they may well have been Egyptian. Others were firmly convinced that the visitors were members of the early Christian Church, some say Saint Thomas himself.[3] Once more it need not concern us here whether these reports are based on actual events or are merely folk legends. Their importance lies in the fact that during the first decades of the sixteenth century the natives of Mexico were telling a tale very similar to the one told by the Utopians to Hythlodaeus.

The Map of Utopia
Two versions of the map appear in the CW edition of *Utopia*. The first appeared in the editon of *Utopia* published in 1516; the second, a more sophisticated version of the first, was included in the 1518 Basle edition. The first artist is unknown but it is thought that the second was drawn by Ambrosius Holbein.[4] A very similar map appeared in Europe to accompany the letters written by Hernán Cortes, telling of the Conquest of Mexico. This map was said to be of the Aztec capital Tenochtitlan.[5] This also appeared in two different versions, the first being attributed to Cromberger who became the first publisher in the New World; the second, more sophisticated version, is thought to have been by one of the Durer brothers. Both are said to have been based on an original map provided by Cortes.[6] We could perhaps accept that the city map with its circular outline did give a reasonable

representation of the shape of the island-city but for one thing. Another map included with the Cortes letter also had this circular form when the area depicted, the Gulf of Mexico and surrounding lands, could not be seen as circular.[7]

Yet another circular map is included in the *Relaciones* depicting an area in the Yucatan and from an investigation of this by Scholes and Roys we learn:

> An unusual feature of the Alfaro map is its highly conventionalised circular outline, although the subject matter does not call for such a form. In this respect it resembles two colonial Yucatecan Indian maps. . . . Since the only circular European maps known to us are those of a hemisphere of the world, where such an outline was required by the subject matter, the junior author of this study has elsewhere expressed the belief that the Yucatan maps followed a native Maya convention. Although the Tabasco map is ascribed to Alfaro [in the *Relacione*] its style suggests the possibility either that he had a native map before him when he drew this chart or that an Indian collaborator, familiar with the Maya convention, aided him in his work.[8]

This circular style of map drawing is called T'ho, a name taken from the Maya name for the city of Merida. Could this explain why the Utopian map bears no resemblance to the physical description of the island contained in the text? Was Peter Giles given a T'ho style map to have copied for the purpose of defining Utopia?

The Utopian Alphabet

Thomas More is not credited with the invention or inclusion of the Utopian alphabet. It was Peter Giles who forwarded this plus the marginal comments and the poem directly to the publisher. Erasmus is thought to have made the marginal notes but no author is credited with the invention of the alphabet or language.[9] It consists of a series of twenty-two irregular geometric shapes, each of which was said to represent a letter in our alphabet. In the Paris edition of 1529 an additional shape was added to represent the letter 'Z'.

The inclusion of an alphabet which could be used to form the basis of a universal language is not surprising in a humanist work of this period. Christian humanists saw the invention of such a language as the fulfilment of Holy Scripture to reunite mankind.[10] Looking at this inclusion from the point of view of our comparison means that if we seek a factual people in the New World on whom to base the Utopian nation we must turn to Mexico, the only place in the Americas to use a written language. The Aztec system never reached the degree of sophistication achieved by the Maya. This is not to say that the Utopian alphabet bears any direct relationship with the system of Maya glyph writing. It is quite simply a reassertion that a factual account of Maya achievements may have influenced the features attributed to More's 'fictional' nation of Utopia.

Bishop Landa wrote a chapter on the Maya alphabet but unfortunately due to linguistic confusion between him and his informant it did not turn out to be a Maya Rosetta Stone. He said that each shape represented a distinct sound, but sounds can also be words that mean different things in different languages. For example, when he asked what the sign for 't' was (pronounced *tay* in Castilian), the informant gave him the word for 'te' (Maya for tree). With the swift adoption of the new alphabet and the total destruction of books written in glyphs the natives lost the ability to read the glyphs very quickly. At the rate scholars are working now to decipher them it should only be a matter of a few more years before another breakthrough occurs.

The language used by More in the text of *Utopia* has been thoroughly researched by Surtz and Hexter among others, seeking to define the roots used in place names, titles etc. Past studies have been complicated by the knowledge that More and Erasmus invented words for inclusion in the text. More in a letter to Giles wrote that many of the names, which appear ridiculous or absurd, were imposed on him by his desire for historical accuracy.[11] If we turn to some of these names such as

'Nephlogetes' we learn that it signifies 'cloud begotten'.[12] The Mixtec, a Mexican group who invaded the Maya, were said to be children of the clouds. (Mix in Nahuatl means cloud.)[13] Could More have sought Greek and Latin roots that most closely approximated names given to him? The name he chose for his Utopian élite was 'Barzanes' which is interpreted as 'adopted or natural sons of Zeus'.[14] As we have seen the Maya élite also traced their descent back to a deified figure, Quetzalcoatl. Throughout Mexico the expression 'sons of Quetzalcoatl' signified those who were rich or successful.[15] One final example, the Utopian capital city Amaurotum translates as darkling or ghostly city. In the notes to the *Popul Vuh* written by Recinos we learn that the legendary city of Xibalba, the ghostly city, was frequently associated with the actual city of Palenque.[16]

This is not just a fanciful exercise. In order to make the comparison it has been essential to disregard past interpretations of the work and assume that More was not jesting when he said he was constrained by his desire for historical accuracy.

The 'Parerga' (decorative artwork)
The drawings that appeared in the CW edition reproduce work from the early editions of *Utopia*.[17] The form some of these have taken raises some intriguing questions when related to this comparison. Erasmus wrote in great detail of the importance attached to the selection of symbols or devices used as trade-marks.[18] We can assume therefore that the same care went into the selection of devices used in *Utopia*. Amongst those chosen were a snake, a bird and a tree, not an unusual inclusion in a humanist work as the snake/caduceus has a very ancient history. The remarkable thing is the combination of snake/bird/tree also has great significance in Mexican culture. The question to ask is whether Marten, Froben and Holbein used these symbols before the publication of *Utopia*? We are told in the CW notes that the publisher, Marten, only used this trademark between 1515 and 1517 after which it was dropped,[19] yet Erasmus said that such devices were not chosen

lightly. The use of bird/air and snake/earth as related symbols is universal so that their appearance in Mexico need not surprise us. What is remarkable is that they were specifically chosen for the first editions of *Utopia* then apparently dropped.

CONCLUSION

CHAPTER 17

Raphael Hythlodaeus

Let us summon Raphael, the heavenly physician, to free us with
ethics and dialectics as with health bringing medicines.
                                          Pico Della Mirandola

Although the strength or weakness of this book must lie
ultimately on the textual comparison between *Utopia* and
existing Maya records, a number of other factors must be
looked at in order to account for our continued acceptance of
the work as a fictional creation of More. The literary evidence
available on the history of the early voyages of discovery
demonstrates that some Europeans knew of the existence of the
Maya before *Utopia* was written. In theory therefore, information on their civilization could have been available to More or
his associates before 1517. The textual comparison has shown a
much higher degree of similarity than can be accounted for by
the creative genius of the author. Despite the strength of the
argument proposing a wholly Old World inspiration for the
customs and institutions of Utopia a New World source was
also possible.

   Was a character like Hythlodaeus also possible? Contrary to
popular belief the early voyages of discovery were not all
undertaken by men motivated by greed and avarice. A great
number of these were made by men S.E. Morison describes as
humanist, gentlemen explorers, motivated by the expansion of
knowledge and curiosity.[1] These men were content to explore
and learn without exploiting. There has been some speculation
that More could have heard tales of the New World through

humanists with a first-hand contact with explorers of this kind. The strongest candidate would be the Spanish humanist, Juan Luis Vives, based mainly on the fact that he and More developed a very close friendship at a later date. Once more Erasmus of Rotterdam provided the link between his two friends. Research into Vives life does not, however, support the claim that he could have been More's informant on New World customs. Although Erasmus and Vives exchanged letters before the publication of *Utopia* there is no mention in these of the new lands or of discoveries being made, nor is there anything to indicate that More even knew of Vives at this stage.[2] Both the letters of Erasmus and of Vives have been well researched in the past as has the friendship between More and Vives. It is felt, therefore, that if a connection existed linking any of these to the publication of *Utopia* it would have come to light before this.

It has also been suggested that Erasmus, through his contacts with the Spanish Court, could have been the one to obtain information to include in *Utopia*. Peter Martyr de Anglieri, who served at court and on the Council for the Indies, is reputed to have known more detail of the new lands and their people than any other person in Europe. Although Martyr did not visit these lands himself he was, in his capacity as councillor, responsible for taking reports from everyone returning from the Indies. Unfortunately none of his letters before 1517 appears to have included details of any society comparable to the Maya.[3] Given Erasmus's contacts at the Spanish Court the total lack of letters that mention the New World is perhaps more surprising than would have been their presence. If the known or speculated sources lead nowhere that leaves us once more with the text of *Utopia* and the claims made by More. The character Raphael Hythlodaeus was described in *Utopia* as an elderly, bearded man of simple appearance. He came from a Portuguese family of some wealth and standing. He was said by Giles to be a scholar of some note who was well versed in Latin, excelled in Greek and as a philosopher compared favourably with Plato.

Some years previously he had signed over his estates in Portugal to his brothers and decided to dedicate his life to exploration. He, it is claimed, sailed on three of the four voyages of the Genoese explorer Amerigo Vespucci (1499–1503). On the fourth and last voyage he won the grudging approval of Vespucci to remain on the mainland of Gulike with twenty-three companions to explore the area. It is from this base that, after a great deal of travel, Hythlodaeus and five companions at last arrived at the land of the Utopians. Hythlodaeus, having decided that Utopia was the most equitable and wisely-governed society he had ever encountered, resolved to spend the rest of his life there.

After a stay of at least five years Hythlodaeus decided he would make one last trip to Europe to tell of the excellent customs and laws evolved by the Utopians. By stages he made his way back to his home port and upon arrival found that he and his companions had long been given up for dead.[4] As we have seen, it was during this trip More claimed to have met the explorer.

Was this fact or fiction? Here once again More had combined verifiable data with claims that have not as yet been verified. The verifiable historical details given are the obvious starting point. Here, as with so much research on *Utopia* we are faced with contradiction and paradox. Investigation of Amerigo Vespucci's life and voyages is far from straightforward. No one, Columbus included, has created more acrimonious debate and academic controversy than the man who gave his name to the new continent of the Americas. On one side are those who claim Vespucci was no more than an arrant/arrogant liar who robbed Columbus and others of their due recognition.[5] On the other are those who see Vespucci as a skilled, experienced navigator who has been sorely maligned by the jealousy and lies of his detractors.[6] The journal mentioned in the text of *Utopia* describes what Vespucci claims were his four journeys to the New World. Two were undertaken on behalf of the Portuguese Court, and two for the Spanish. Serious doubts have been raised over whether he did in fact ever make the first and fourth voyages or merely related the experiences of others who had.

This debate has raged since the first publication of Vespucci's reports. In 1812 in response to an enquiry from Spain, the head archivist to the Kingdom of Portugal, one Vizconde de Santaren, replied that after a thorough search of all documents related to the Portuguese voyages of discovery between 1497 and 1632 he could trace only the briefest mention of Vespucci. This record referred to a meeting between the explorer Cabral and Vespucci on the Cape Verde Isles. The archivist had also researched all exchange of documents between the Spanish and Portuguese Courts and found no mention of Vespucci.[7]

Knowing that this controversy was raging around Europe when *Utopia* was written one must ask whether More included specific mention of Vespucci to further cloud the issue. A non-existent island discovered on a non-existent voyage? Or, like many of More's little jests, does this one also have a deeper significance? Are there clues to be found either in the text of *Utopia* or in the Vespucci account?

In the report of the fourth voyage made by Vespucci we learn that he was not the leader, merely one of the navigators.[8] In the Utopian text we are told that Hythlodaeus sailed 'not like Palinurus but Ulyssis'. Palinurus was the navigator of Captain Aeneas's ship who nearly lost the vessel through negligence. Ulyssis was, like Aeneas, the captain of his vessel. If we return to the Vespucci account we find that the captain of the fleet on the fourth voyage was, like Hythlodaeus, a Portuguese.[9] The name of the captain was Gonzalo de Coellho, the son of a prominent Portuguese family, who had earned a reputation as a much respected and experienced explorer long before the fourth voyage of Vespucci. On the 1504–5 Maillo map of the new lands Coellho's name appears on the area of Brazil as the first man to discover and explore these lands. He, opponents of Vespucci claim, is one of the more worthy men robbed of their due recognition by a boastful liar.[10] The Genoese makes no secret in his letters that he thought he was much better suited to the command of the fleet than this gentleman, humanist explorer. Cowardly, swollen-headed and presumptious are just some of the words Vespucci used to describe the captain. The cowardly label was applied because Coellho refused to give Vespucci and a few like-minded companions, permission to commit wholesale slaughter of some natives as reprisal for the killing of one of their companions.[11]

In the Vespucci report of the fourth voyage we are told of men who remained behind on the Brazilian coast. In contrast to the Utopian account, Vespucci was more than glad to leave them as after the sinking of Coellho's flagship he was reluctant to overload his own ship with the captain's crew for the return voyage to Europe. More's inclusion of Vespucci's reluctance could be construed as a touch of irony given the facts as stated in the Vespucci journal. Coellho did write a book of his experiences in the new lands which he dedicated to King Juan III of Portugal, but unfortunately this is lost. The last account of Coellho that can be traced in the Spanish archives is of his leaving on 10 June 1506, with a fleet of six ships for the Americas.[12] Even if it cannot be established that Coellho was the prototype for Hythlodaeus his story by its inclusion in the Vespucci reference demonstrates that a character such as the one described by More did exist.

CHAPTER 18

Motives for Fictional Interpretations in the Sixteenth Century

... chroniclers ... persist in the belief ... that the indigenes were irrational simply because they did not experience christian revelation. The time has come to acknowledge and study the manifestations ... replete with truths of divine revelation.

Vila Selma

... things that once would have seemed permissable or even salutary came to [More] dangerous.

C.S. Lewis

We must now turn to what could prove to be the most difficult problem posed by this interpretation of *Utopia*. Why have the questions raised here not been raised previously? We have already discussed the reasons why past interpreters have classified the work as pure fiction and, compelling as these are, a serious study of New World influences would at the very least have shaken the cast-iron faith in the purely fictional nature of the work sufficiently to inspire additional research. Other more compelling reasons must exist that have discouraged a study such as this.

The first and most obvious reason is that, even if the events leading up to the writing of the book did transpire exactly as More says they did, perhaps Thomas More and his associates did not believe the traveller's tales were factual. Although

intrigued and hopeful they may have concluded that such a
society was just too good to be true, a romanticized noble
savage story. They could have decided to wait and see if future
explorers also returned with stories that confirmed Hythlodaeus' account. If this was the case they would have waited
in vain. After the 'official' discovery of the Maya, tales of the
well-run and ordered Maya society paled into insignificance
alongside the tales of gold beyond belief in a nation that not
only practised human sacrifice but cannabilism as well. No one
would have accepted that the peoples to be found in this new
land of Mexico were not all of the same nature. When these
stories started to circulate from 1517 More and his fellow
humanists may well have been convinced that Hythlodaeus
was playing a joke on them with his tale of a well and
wisely-run republic.

Another reason for the true nature of the work never being
revealed may lie in the motivation of the author. A great deal
has been written on the idealistic motivation of More in
seeking to present his image of the ideal state, but very little
has been said about possible commercial benefits that could
have arisen. The former opinions are perfectly in keeping with
our recent view of Saint Thomas More, but the man was not a
saint when he wrote the work and there is nothing dishonour-
able in being motivated by profit. Biographies of More show
that although he was reputed to be above taking bribes in his
official capacity, he was just as interested as the next man of his
generation in seeking rewards and profit. His involvement
with the world of commerce is well documented and one of his
avowed aims in producing the book was reputedly to show it
to Cardinal Wolsey.[1] Perhaps this was because he saw the
potential for national and personal profit in trade with these
new lands. It is surely a strange coincidence that the only
record we have of a planned expedition from England to these
new lands in this period was made by Thomas More's
brother-in-law, John Rastell. Rastell would appear to have
been cast in the mould of the great entrepreneurs, always on
the lookout for ways to consolidate his fortune. He wrote a

play based on the new lands called *The Four Seasons*. This deals almost exclusively with the profits to be made trading in the New World.

Rastell set out in 1517 to make his fortune in the new lands. From the outset his expedition was beset by problems and finally had to be abandoned on the coast of Ireland. Rastell claimed that the failure was due to sabotage and instigated a costly and lengthly court battle to sue the rich and powerful men he claimed were responsible for his failure.[2] Is it possible that these rich and powerful men could have been the ones mentioned earlier who were said to trade in the New World? The failure of Rastell's mission could well have spelled the end of More's interest in the New World. We do know that after the 1518 Basle edition of the work More showed no further interest in promoting it.

General interest in the work does not appear to have wained as between 1518 and 1520 four more editions were published.[3] Erasmus of Rotterdam continued his interest in the book and it has been said that his interest was always greater than More's. By these dates Erasmus had even more compelling reasons for not disclosing a factual basis for the work. In the prevailing climate of religious and political strife Erasmus was finding it very difficult to avoid either supporting or denying Martin Luther who had precipitated it. This neutral position earned him the emnity of many powerful Church figures and accusations of promoting Arianism. To announce at this stage that the peoples described in *Utopia* were an actual society would have been foolhardy in the extreme. Two features of Utopian society would have created a furore that would have made that caused by Luther insignificant by comparison. First we are told that they had evolved a communal way of life that offered a more equitable society than any to be found in Europe. Augustine writing in the early fourth century had stated that such communal life, though the ideal sought by Christ, could never be attained by mankind, and the succeeding Church fathers reiterated the same opinions.[4] If someone such as Erasmus had declared to the contrary it would have shaken the foundations of the Church. The second feature of Utopian society that would have created uproar was that the Utopians believed man could arrive at a knowledge of the one god through the use of reason combined with a study of nature. The divinity of Christ and the Scriptures are the bedrock of the Christian Church and to question this in the sixteenth century would have led to accusations of heresy and a possible death sentence. By Erasmus' own admission he was not of the stuff from which martyrs are made.[5] There was nothing to be gained and much to be lost by claiming a factual basis for Utopian society.

L.K. Born has drawn attention to the fact that in Erasmus's work *Insitutio principis Christiani* he incorporated thirty points that were to appear in the later published *Utopia*; some have even christened this work *The Political Utopia*.[6] Perhaps the time has come to reassess all Erasmus's work to see if his life, not More's, should be researched for possible New World connections. *Utopia* was never intended for wide readership, in fact the thought of it being translated into English was enough to arouse Thomas More to declare to Erasmus that he would rather see the book burned than expose it to the readership and misinterpretations of a less educated public.[7] More's fears were not without foundation. The writings of Bartolome de Las Casas telling of the atrocities and cruelties in the Americas were circulated widely and used as anti-Spanish and anti-Rome propaganda.[8] *Utopia* might well have taken this a step further into anti-Christian propaganda.

According to Richard Eden, in what is claimed as the first European history of the Americas, Erasmus had a great interest in the New World and had intended writing on the theme in the same style as Martin a Goes. Unfortunately he died before realizing this ambition.[9] Any work he had written would doubtless, like *Utopia*, have been destined for a very restricted readership. Erasmus, perhaps even more than More, believed that true knowledge should be kept in the hands of intellectuals. It was their duty to interpret and pass on the message to the less learned as they saw fit. Therefore, it is felt that even if Erasmus had been aware of a factual basis in *Utopia* he would never have made this widely known.

Epilogue

As long as harmony is preserved at home and its institutions are in
a healthy state, not all the envy of neighbouring rulers . . . can
avail to shatter or shake that nation.

Utopia

. . . with the help of God, I will enter your country by force; I
will carry on war against you with the utmost violence; I will
subject you to the yoke of obedience, to the church and King; I
will take your wives and children and make slaves of them, . . . all
the bloodshed and calamities which shall follow are to be imputed
to you and not to his majesty, or to me, or those who serve under
me . . .

Spanish proclamation

The initial objective of this work was to lay before the reader
evidence which would at least indicate some possibility that a
work of world renown such as *Utopia* could be founded on fact.
The evidence has been presented and the verdict is now with
the reader.

During the past seven years of gathering the evidence which
is now put forward to support the theory of a factual base for
Utopia, I have come to know both the content of that work and
the historical background to the Maya in great detail. It is
hard to believe that in the more than four hundred and seventy
years which have passed since the book first appeared, no one
has seriously challenged the interpretation of *Utopia* as a work
of fiction.

My admiration for the Maya was first kindled during a
two-year stay in Mexico and has been enhanced by the reading
done for this book. Their general degree of advancement was
equal if not greater than that achieved in ancient Greece, and
they had the advantage in that their civilization survived until

the arrival of the Europeans. Most histories of the Americas since the advent of the Europeans make very depressing and tragic reading from the indigenous people's point of view. The one ray of light that shines out from modern studies of the Maya is that the general character of the people would appear to have changed very little over the past five hundred years of occupation. It would also appear that the age-old custom of the Mayanization of outsiders is still going on. Those who choose to reside among the Maya very soon find that they too begin to think and feel like their hosts.

Even with a limited background knowledge of the Maya the parallels between Utopian and Amerindian life leapt at me from the pages of *Utopia*. No doubt some of the details of the ideal society have been manipulated by More to get a particular message across, but the similarities between More's 'fictional' state and the actual situation of the Maya at the same point in history forces one to ask if it could all be coincidence that More included fairly obscure or rare features that both share.

The geographical similarities, the description of the lagoon with navigational aids, the social stratification, the artificial hatcheries, the feather cloaks, secret knowledge that had to be passed on, euthanasia, the unusual wedding custom, married and female priests – some of these features may have been found in other states, imaginary or real, but it is a strange coincidence that finds them all located in one source. I can see no logic in arguing that More would have collated these details from hundreds of sources to formulate his ideal state when it can be shown that a contemporary society offered a single living example.

Ascribing a fictional interpretation to *Utopia* has become a tradition and we do not give up our traditions lightly. To continue to insist on *Utopia* as fiction is not entirely logical when most of those doing the literary interpretation know only one side of the issue, the views and environment of the Northern humanists, and little or nothing of the other side comprised by the New World and its people. It can only be presumed that prior comparisons have not been made due to an inherent tendency in the academic world towards over-specialization. Questions raised in one area of study, such as literature, are not answered in another, such as history. Now that we know much more of the history and traditions of the Amerindian we should at least re-examine texts such as *Utopia* with an open mind. It is freely acknowledged that More had access to earlier travel tales, these too should be re-examined in the light of the wealth of evidence emerging for a pre-Columbian knowledge of the Americas.

Any attempt to ascribe a factual basis to *Utopia* is seen as a personal attack on Thomas More's integrity or creative genius. Irrespective of the source of his material the issues raised by More in *Utopia* are timeless and universal concerns of mankind. The fears engendered in sixteenth-century Europe are not so different from the ones that would be raised now if it could be established that Utopia did exist and was destroyed by Europeans. If there is any foundation to this claim do we not owe it to the Maya, and the other civilizations we destroyed, to try and give them back a history they should be proud of?

Utopia and/or the Maya can teach us a great deal even in our present stage of development not only with regard to our attitude towards the earth's resources and their conservation but also in the art of living in peace with other nations, the application of self-discipline, moderation in all things and the effect of exposure to cruel and violent acts. All these are matters of concern to all of us today.

Not least of the lessons we could learn would be that of religious toleration. A look at the world today would show wars being fought in many areas in the name of religion. Is it important what name we give to our God, or whether we even have one? Shortly after the publication of *Utopia* Erasmus risked being branded as a heretic when he wrote:

How much more in accord with Christ's teaching it is to regard the whole world as one household . . . think of all mankind as brethren . . . not to examine where a man lives but how well he lives . . .[1]

The Maya used very similar words to describe their nation to the Spaniards, the nation lived as one household, we were the homebreakers. We should not be afraid to confront our past.

If we allow fear to govern our interpretation of any historical text then we vindicate those who label historians as the purveyors of ideals and interpretations that do not threaten the *status quo* of the society they form part of. Academic pride also plays its part in interpretation:

> . . . what is accessible in a book depends on the conventional
> expectation of its readers, and (that) those conventions are
> maintained by institutions, the Church in one era, the universities
> in another. Academic traditionalists protest loudly at this. They
> resent being told that their eternal truths are in fact local customs
> . . . customs that blind them to much that authors put in their
> books . . .[2]

One could add to this that some of the authors, for reasons of their own, contribute to the blinding. Perhaps in publishing *Utopia* Thomas More and his associates have done the greatest service to a still extant people, the Maya, than has ever been done for them since Europeans entered their country in force. The adoption of many of the Maya/Utopian practices may be our only chance of saving a planet we failed to love and cherish as they did. We, like them, should consider ourselves not the owners of the earth but its guardians.

Budé, one of the rich and powerful men to whom More sent a copy of *Utopia*, wrote in a letter:

> Our age and future ages will have this history as a precious source
> of noble and useful laws which each one may take and adopt to the
> use of his own state.[3]

Notes

Abbreviations

CW   *The Yale Edition of the Complete Works of Saint Thomas More. Volume Four: Utopia.* New Haven and London. Yale University Press. 1965.

DHM   *Coleccion de Documentos para la historia de Mexico*; 2 vols. Edited and published by J. Garcia Icazbalcete. Mexico. 1858–66.

CDI–1   *Coleccion de Documentos ineditos. Relativos al Descubrimiento, conquista y organizacion de las Antiquas Posesiones espanoles de America y Oceana. Sacados de los Archivos de Reino y muy especialmente del Indias. Completamente autorizada.* First series. 42 vols. Madrid. 1864–84.

CDI–2   *Coleccion de Documentos ineditos. Relativos al Descubrimiento, conquista y organizacion de las Antiquas Posesiones espanoles de Ultramar.* Second series. 25 vols. Madrid. 1885–1932.

RY   *Relaciones de Yucatan.* Volumes 11 and 13 of CDI–2. Madrid. 1898–1900.

SW   *The Yale Edition of the Selected Works of Saint Thomas More.* Ed. E. Surtz SJ, based on the translation by G.C. Richards. New Haven and London. Yale University Press. 1964.

3 Past Interpretations of *Utopia*

1 CW, ciiii–cixxx
2 Lewis 1954, 169
3 CW, xxxi
4 CW, 49
5 CW, 274
6 CW, 10
7 Graves 1960, 354–7
8 Harpsfield and Roper 1978, 110

9   Stapleton 1966, 127
10 Ferguson 1975
11 CW, 41 Letter from More to Giles

4   Confusion over Dating

1   Navarrete 1825, 434
2   Diaz del Castillo 1982, 25–54
3   Morison 1974
4   Ruz Menendez 1976
5   Irving 1866, 291; Morison 1974, 241
6   Columbus 1960, ed. Vigneras, notes xv–xviii
7   CDI–1 38, 239–40
8   CDI–1 19, 446, 479–83
9   Arciniegas 1959, 12–36; Irving 1866, 130–1
10 CDI–1 8, 33–61. There are collections of documents from several sittings of these hearings held on both sides of the Atlantic in other volumes but all consulted contain the Maya question and the comments added to the Cuba document.
11 Quinn 1973, 19
12 Roukema 1956, 30–8
13 *Croyland Chronicle* 1854, 474
14 Eden 1971, 59
15 Quinn 1973, 11
16 Scenna 1974, 145
17 CW 280, 295

5   Early Voyages

1   Martyr 1990, letter 168 57 dated 5–10–1496
2   CW 341
3   Torquemada 1975, 352
4   Landa 1982, 4–5
5   Irving 1866, 281
6   Martyr cited Torres Asensio 1892, 51
7   Morison 1974, 208
8   Parry 1971, 261
9   DHM 1858, 281–308
10 Diaz del Castillo 1982, 46, 71
11 Diaz del Castillo 1982, 81

12 Diaz del Castillo 1982, 27
13 Dias del Castillo 1982, 46
14 CW 51 Vespucci 1983, 93–4
15 Columbus 1960, 134
16 CDI–1 39, 429
17 Diaz del Castillo 1882, 69–70
18 Cortes 1982, 21
19 Landa 1982, 229–30
20 Coleccion de Salazar MS 145, fol. 15. Academia Real, Madrid; CDI–2 11, 306, 312
21 Landa 1982, 139–40
22 Altamira 1962, 283
23 CDI–1 34, 291–3
24 CW 51, 53

6 Sources Used

1 Robertson 1869, vol. 6, 343–5, vol. 7, 247–81
2 Lopez Estrada 1965, 27–40; Zavala 1977, 302–11
3 Landa 1982, 7
4 Cook and Borah 1966, cited Parry 1971, 213–20
5 Las Casas 1983, 17. Even at the time of writing Las Casas thought the figure was nearer fifteen million.

7 The Island of Utopia

1 CW 113
2 Prescott 1854, vol. 2, 514–17
3 Landa 1982, 3
4 RY II–11, 347; Scholes and Roys 1968, 50, 458
5 CW 111, 113
6 Thompson 1956, 27–8
7 CW 111
8 CW 111
9 Orosa Diaz 1945, 70
10 Diaz del Castillo 1982, 43
11 RY II–11, 344–7; Chapman 1957, 114–53
12 RY II–11, 374; Landa 1982, 5, 221
13 CW 111
14 Henderson 1981, 226; Thompson 1956, 112–13
15 CW 113

16 *Popul Vuh* 1982, 164; *Chilam Balam* 1982, 154
17 RY II–13, 162; Landa 1982, 13; *Popul Vuh* 1982, 153–4
18 CW 113
19 Thompson 1956, 75
20 Henderson 1981, 145–6
21 Torquemada 1975, 344
22 RY II–13, 22
23 RY II–13, 19
24 CW 113
25 Godoy and Olmo 1979, 184
26 CW 115, 125
27 Landa 1982, 40, 57
28 Coe 1973, 170
29 Henderson 1981, 150
30 Rivera Dorado 1982, 39, passim; Landa 1982, 14
31 CW 115
32 Billingsley 1980, 80; Derrett 1966, 61–5
33 Lorenz 1952, XV
34 Sahagun 1982, 519, passim
35 Torquemada 1975, 406
36 CW 117
37 *Chilam Balam* 1982, 192–3
38 Landa 1982, 36
39 CW 117
40 RY II–13, 47, 185
41 Rivera Dorado 1982, 55–72
42 Landa 1982, 14
43 CW 117
44 Landa 1982, 35, 40, 205–6

8 The Cities

1 CW 113, 115, 117, 119
2 Thompson 1956, 32–5
3 CW 119
4 Thompson 1956, 73
5 Sahagun 1982, 203
6 CW 119
7 *Popul Vuh* 1982, 136–7
8 Cortes 1982, 250–1

9   CW 121

10 Torquemada 1975, 342

11 Landa 1982, 11

12 Cortes 1982, 266–7; Gomara 1985, 252–4

13 Landa 1982, 228

14 CW 121

15 Landa 1982, 34

16 CW 121

17 Landa 1982, 111

18 CW 121; Landa 1982, 228; Anon Con 1964, 160

19 RY II–13, 35; Landa 1982, 28

20 Roys cited Rivera Dorado 1982, 40

21 Diaz del Castillo 1982, 51

22 CW 137

23 Landa 1982, 11, 107

24 CW 135, 137

25 Landa 1982, 18; Sahagun 1982, 611

26 CW 245

27 CW 121. CW 120, lines 26–7, 'Quos ab capta usque insula . . .', are not translated on CW 121. The Robinson translation 1908, 92, reads, '. . . even from the first conquest of the island . . .'.

28 Rivera Dorado 1982, 332

29 CW 121. CW 120ff states that the 1517 edition had the word 'alnum'. CW 133 tells of the preparation of timber for construction. The Robinson translation 1908, 93, reads, '. . . and the inner sides be well strengthened with timber . . .'.

30 Thompson 1956, 78–85

31 CW 121, 123

32 Thompson 1956, 83; Henderson 1981, 184, 221

33 Landa 1982, 106

9   **Political Organizations**

1 CW 123, 125

2 RY II–13, 182, 211

3 Scholes and Roys 1968, 35

4 Scholes and Roys 1968, 55–6, Rivera Dorado 1982, 180–4

5 *Popul Vuh* 1982, 157

6 Scholes and Roys 1968, 87, passim

7 CW 113, 123, 133

8 Thompson 1956, 111
9 Scholes and Roys 1968, 60–7
10 Scholes and Roys 1968, 51–2, passim
11 Scholes and Roys 1968, 61

10 Social customs

1 CW 185, passim
2 Rivera Dorado 1982, 192; Henderson 1981, 62–3
3 Landa 1982, 67
4 Lopez de Gomara 1985, 251–2
5 Landa 1982, 17–18
6 Rivera Dorado 1982, 45
7 CW 129
8 Landa 1982, 15
9 CW 133, 135
10 *Chilam Balam* 1982, 50, 63
11 RY II–13, 49, 189
12 Sahagun 1982, 603, 606
13 CW 127
14 Landa 1982, 60–1
15 Sahagun 1982, 460
16 Prescott 1854, vol. 2, 264ff.
17 CW 113, 133, 135, 137. The Robinson translation 1908, 103, states 'and the commonwealth in good stay . . .', which suggests that a defined point is reached before a halt is called to construction.
18 Thompson 1956, 91–7

11 Population Control

1 CW 135, 137
2 CW 414–15
3 Thompson 1956, 37–8
4 Aguilar 1977, 66–76, 101–2
5 RY II–13, 30, 48, 189
6 *Popul Vuh* 1982, 127–62
7 Thompson 1956, 118
8 Henderson 1981, 195
9 *Chilam Balam* 1982, 21–5
10 Thompson 1956, 91, 94
11 CW 137, 139; Scholes and Roys 1968, 54

12 Landa 1982, 40; Cortes 1982, 71
13 Henderson 1981, 149
14 CW 139
15 Chapman 1957, 114–53
16 CW 139
17 Landa 1982, 88, passim; Torquemada 1975, 283
18 CW 139
19 *Popul Vuh* 1982, 158–9, passim
20 Thompson 1956, 111
21 CW 139, 141
22 Cortes 1982, 245; Von Hagan 1973, 218
23 Landa 1982, 14, 42

12 Trade

1 CW 145, 147
2 Landa 1982, 203–19
3 CW 147
4 CW 147, 149
5 Henderson 1981, 152
6 Rivera Dorado 1982, 54–60
7 CW 149
8 Cortes 1982, 248; Rivera Dorado 1982, 68; Scholes and Roys 1968, 29–31, 59; Chapman 1957, 114–53
9 CW 153, 155, 571
10 Martyr cited Eden 1971, 117, 120, 152, 189; Landa 1982, 231
11 CW 169
12 RY II–13, 183; Diaz del Castillo 1982, 46, passim
13 Col. de Salazar MS 145, fol. 15. Academia Real.
14 CW 159
15 Scholes and Roys 1968, 12, 60; Landa 1982, 11
16 CW 159
17 RY II–13, 352
18 Vila Selma 1981, 34
19 Coe 1973, 36–42
20 CW 159, 161, 163, 183
21 Thompson 1956, 23, 144
22 Thompson 1956, 151–4
23 Landa 1982, 60
24 CW 161, 163

25 CW 139, 171
26 Landa 1982, 74–5
27 RY II–13, 193, 217
28 *Chilam Balam* 1982, 71–3, passim; Thompson 1956, 100, 114–15, 237–44
29 CW 179, 181
30 Landa 1982, 35, 37, 41; Robertson 1869, vol. 6, 266–77
31 CW 179
32 Landa 1982, 117
33 Turner 1981, 285
34 Gowlett 1984, 170–1; Rivera Dorado 1982, 20, 26
35 CW 179, 183
36 RY II–13, 47, 188, 208; Landa 1982, 4
37 *Chilam Balam* 1982, 192–3
38 RY II–13, 47, 188, 208; Landa 1982, 4
39 CW 181
40 Prescott 1854, vol. 2, 390
41 CW 183, 185
42 Sahagun 1982, 583
43 Landa 1982, 105
44 Von Hagan 1973, 220–2

13 Slavery

1 CW 193
2 Scholes and Roys 1968, 56, 58–9
3 Cortes 1982, 29
4 Diaz del Castillo 1982, 78–9
5 RY II–13, 44
6 Rivera Dorado 1982, 123; Landa 1982, 53
7 CW 187
8 Robertson 1869, vol. 6, 369–70
9 Sahagun 1982, 600
10 *Chilam Balam* 1982, 73; *Popul Vuh* 1982, notes 169–70
11 Landa 1982, 60; Vaillent 1978, 179
12 CW 237
13 CW 186, 476
14 *Chilam Balam* 1982, 9–10, passim
15 CW 233

16 Stephens 1962, vol. I, 142–5, 263; Stephens 1969, vol. II, 359–61, 371–2
17 CW 187, 189, 191
18 Landa 1982, 42
19 Prescott 1854, vol. 1, 127
20 CW 187, 189
21 Sahagun 1982, 362–6
22 Rivera Dorado 1982, 82–3
23 CW 193
24 Landa 1982, 17
25 Rivera Dorado 1982, 152, 154
26 CW 195
27 *Chilam Balam* 1982, notes 182; Landa 1982, 217–18
28 *Popul Vuh* 1982, 103–4
29 Vila Selma 1981, 43, 73; Rivera Dorado 1982, 50
30 Diaz del Castillo 1982, 32, passim
31 CW 195
32 Rivera Dorado 1982, 186–8
33 Thompson 1956, 139–40
34 Las Casas 1983, 59
35 CW 197
36 Henderson 1981, 153

14 Warfare

1 CW 215
2 Diaz del Castillo 1982, 43
3 *Popul Vuh* 1982, 138
4 Diaz del Castillo 1982, 42. The Spanish forces that conquered Peru used Mexican armour; Hemming 1972, 42
5 CW 215
6 CW 201
7 Rivera Dorado 1982, 65–71; Sahagun 1982, 498–500
8 CW 201
9 *Chilam Balam* 1982, 22–33; Landa 1982, 15–19. The Utopian war was said to have destroyed their faith in formal leagues. CW 199. The defeat of Mayapan led to the disbanding of the Mayapan league.
10 CW 203
11 Robertson 1869, vol. 6, 322–40, 378, passim
12 CW 205, 207, 209

13 Landa 1982, 16–17; Stephens 1962, vol. I, 325; *Chilam Balam* 1982, 22
14 CW 203
15 Vaillent 1978, 127, 214–24
16 CW 209, 211, 213
17 RY II–13 186; Landa 1982, 49, 52
18 CW 201, 209, 211
19 Landa 1982, 56
20 CW 211
21 Thompson 1956, 118; Stephens, 1962 vol. I, 23–41
22 Scholes and Roys 1968, 82, 86
23 Coe 1972, 159

15 Religion

1   CW 217
2   Sahagun 1982, 195–7, 202–4; Landa 1982, 16–17; Thompson 1956, 231–2; Rivera Dorado 1982, 65–71
3   Vila Selma 1981, 67; RY II–11, 75
4   Scholes and Roys 1968, 272
5   CW 217
6   Rivera Dorado 1982, 193
7   Thompson 1956, 127
8   CW 217, 219
9   Landa 1982, 44
10 Thompson 1956, 259
11 Landa 1982, 48, 49; Cortes 1982, 30
12 RY II–13, 47; Anon Con 1964, 180
13 DHM 1858, 281–308; Landa 1982, 45, passim
14 CW 223, 225
15 DHM 1858, 281–308; Landa 1982, 59
16 Rivera Dorado 1982, 131, 246
17 CW 227, 229, 231
18 Landa 1982, 18
19 Diaz del Castillo 1982, 170
20 Landa 1982, 14–15, passim; Diaz del Castillo 1982, 164
21 RY II–13, 182; Coe 1973, 179
22 CW 229
23 *Chilam Balam* 1982, 159; Coe 1973, 179
24 Landa 1982, 65, passim

25   CW 231

26   Santos, G. 1981, 29–91; Landa 1982, 70–103; *Chilam Balam* 1982, 194–5

27   Landa 1982, 45, passim

28   CW 235

29   CW 231, 235

30   Thompson 1956, 115

31   CW 233

32   Thompson 1956, 126

33   CW 235. If we accept the Robinson translation 1908, 196, of 'ludis' as plays, we can add this to the pastimes shared by the two nations, Landa writes that the Maya were much addicted to plays; Landa 1982, 38

34   Landa 1982, 93–4

35   Anon Con 1964, 180

36   Landa 1982, 46

37   Landa 1982, 45

38   CW notes 554

39   Eden 1971, 160, 197; Hanke 1968, 317

40   Sahagun 1982, 607–8

41   CW 235

42   *Chilam Balam* 1982, 131–43; Rivera Dorado 1982, 182–3

43   Landa 1982, 39, 83

16   **References to Utopia in Book One of the Text**

1   CW 107

2   CW 109

3   Sahagun 1982. Notes by Carlos Maria Bustamente 981–1000 are reproduced from the 1829/30 edition.

4   CW clxxxiii–clxxxix and notes 276–7

5   Momprade and Gutierrez 1976, 114–15

6   Von Hagan 1973, 79

7   Momprade and Gutierrez 1976, 114–15

8   Scholes and Roys 1968, between pp. 16–17

9   CW 18, 23, 280–1

10   Yates 1971, 163–6, 416–22

11   CW 251

12   CW 500

13   Henderson 1981, 227

14 CW 411
15 Sahagun 1982, 598; Thompson 1956, 105–6
16 *Popul Vuh* 1982, notes 169
17 CW 253, 257
18 Erasmus, Mann–Philips 1967, 5–9
19 CW clxxxv

17 **Raphael Hythlodaeus**

1 Morison 1974, 208
2 Vives 1943, ed. Casanova
3 Eden 1971; Torres Asensio 1892
4 CW 49, 51, 53, 107, 117
5 Morison 1974, 272–312
6 Arciniegas 1959, 12–36
7 CDI–1 39, 531–49
8 Vespucci 1983, 59–94
9 Vespucci 1983, 59–94
10 Morison 1974, 273–318
11 Vespucci 1983, 83–94
12 CDI–1 39, 549

18 **Motives for Fictional Interpretations in the Sixteenth Century**

1 More 1961, ed. Rogers, 90
2 Rastel 1979, notes Axton
3 CW clxxxiii–cxcii
4 CW cv–cxxxiv
5 Demolen 1978, 19–20
6 Cited CW clxxx–clxxxi
7 McConica 1977, 136–49
8 Menendez Pidal 1967, 62–70
9 Eden 1971, 58

19 **Epilogue**

1 Erasmus 1901–18, ed. Nichols, 567–8
2 Mendelson review of Kermode's *Essays on Fiction*, *Sunday Times* 16 Oct. 1983
3 Stapleton 1966, 29. The Budé letter that is reproduced on CW 5–15 does not refer to *Utopia* as a history.

Bibliography

Place of publication is given only if outside London.

Aguilar, F. de, *Relacion breve de la Conquista de la Nueva Espana*. Mexico, U.N.A.M., 1977.

Altamira, R., *A History of Spain*. Lee, M. (trans.). New York, Van Nostrand.

Anderegg, M.A., 'The tradition of early More biography', in R.S. Sylvester and G. Marc'hadour (eds.), *Essential Articles for the Study of Thomas More*. Connecticut, 1977.

Anguera, O. and Moctezuma, M., *Tres Horas con el Arte Maya*. Mexico, Museo Nacional de Antropologia, 1967.

Arciniegas, G., 'Vespucci, una vida malhadada', *Boletin de Historia y Antiguiadades*, vol. XLI, pp. 12–36.

——, 'Amerigo Vespucci and the New World', in Jensen de Lamar (ed.), *The Expansion of Modern Europe*. Boston, D.C. Heath, 1967.

Barker, A.E., 'Clavis Moreana: The Yale Edition of Thomas More', in Sylvester and Marc'hadour (eds.), *Essential Articles*, pp. 229–33.

Bataillon, M., *Erasmus y el Erassmismo*. C. Pujol (Castilian trans.). Barcelona. Editorial Critica, 1977.

Billingsley, D.B., *Pliny, Mandeville and the Utopian Egg Incubation*. Moreana, 1980, no. 67, p. 80.

Bonilla y San Martin, A., *La Filosofia de Renacimiento*. 3 vols. volume 1 *(Vives) El hombre y la Epoca*. Madrid, 1929.

Boxer, C.R., *The Portuguese Seaborne Empire 1415–1825*. Hutchinson & Co. Ltd, 1969.

Chapman, A.M., 'Port of trade enclaves in Aztec and Maya civilisation', in Polanyi, Arensberg and Pearson (eds.), *Trade and Markets in the Early Empires*. Illinois, Free Press, 1957.

Chilam Balam. El Libro de los Libros de Chilam Balam. Barrera Vasquez and Rendon (eds.), Mexico, Fondo de Cultura Economica, 1982.

Coe, M., *The Maya*. Middlesex, Penguin Books, 1973.

Cohen, J.M. (ed. and trans.), *The Four Voyages of Christopher Columbus*. Middlesex, Penguin Books, 1969.

Columbus, C., *The Journal of Christopher Columbus*. A. Vigneras (trans., ed. and notes), Anthony Blond and the Orion Press, 1960.

Cortes, H., *Cartas de Relacion de la Conquista de Mexico*. Madrid, Espasa Calpe, 1982.

Croyland Chronicle. H.T. Riley (ed.), 1854.

Davies, R.T., *Golden Century of Spain, 1501–1621*. Macmillan, 1970.

Demolen, R.L. (ed.), *Essays on the Works of Erasmus*. Yale University Press, 1978.

Derrett, J.D.M., 'Utopia's chickens home to roost', *Moreana*, no. 12, 1981, pp. 61–5.

——, 'The Utopian Alphabet', *Moreana*, no. 77, 1966, pp. 77–8.

——, 'Thomas More and the legislation of the Corporation of London', in Sylvester and Marc'hadour (eds.), *Essential Articles*.

[Diaz, J.], Icazbalceta. (ed.), *Itinerario de Juan Grijalba*. Mexico, Icazbalceta, 1858–66.

Diaz del Castillo, B., *Historia Verdadera de la Conquista de la Nueva Espana*. Madrid, Espasa Calpe, 1982.

Eden, R., *The First Three English Books on America*. (1511–55) Being chiefly translated compilations etc., from the writings and maps of Pedro Martire of Anghiera, 1455–1526; Sebastien Münster, cosmographer, 1489–1515; Sebastian Cabot of Bristol, 1474–1557. 1st edn. Birmingham, 1885, (ed.) Arber, E., F.S.A., New York, Kraus reprint, 1971.

Elliot, J.H., *Imperial Spain, 1492–1716*. New York, St Martin's Press, 1964.

——, *The Old World and the New 1492–1650*. C.U.P., 1970.

Elton, G.R., 'Sir Thomas More and the opposition to Henry VII' in Sylvester and Marc'hadour (eds.), *Essential Articles*, pp. 79–91.

Erasmus, D., *Epistles of Erasmus from His Earliest Letters to His Fifty-First Year*. 3 vols., F.M. Nicholas (ed.), 1901–118.

——, *Adages of Erasmus*. M. Mann-Phillips (ed.), C.U.P. 1964.

——, *Christian Humanism and the Reformation, selected writings of Erasmus*. J.C. Olin (ed.), New York, Fordham University Press, 1976.

——, *Elogio de la Locura*. Madrid, Sarpe, 1984.

Ferguson, J., *Utopias of the Classical World*. 1975.

Fernandez Duro, C., 'Noticias de Yucatan', *Boletin de la Real Academia*, tomo VII, pp. 306–11.

Froude, J.A., *Life and Letters of Erasmus*. Longman, Green & Co., 1906.

Fuentes, P. (ed. and notes), *Anonimous Conquistador. The Conquistadors*. Cassell, 1964.

Gilmour, M.P., *The World of Humanism, 1453–1517*. London, Harper and Row, 1962.

Godoy, R. y Olmo, A., *Textos de Cronistas de Indias y Poemas Precolombinos*. Madrid, Ed. Nacional, 1979.

Gowlet, J., *Ascent to Civilisation. The Archeology of Early Man*. Roxby and Lindsay, 1984.

Graves, R., *The Greek Myths*. 2 vols, Middlesex, Penguin Books, 1957, 1960.

Hadingham, E., *Early Man and the Cosmos*. Heinemann (William) Ltd., 1983.

Hale, J.R., *Renaissance Europe 1480–1520*. Fontana, 1971.

Hanke, L., *Bartolome de Las Casas. An Interpretation of His Life and Writings*. The Hague, Martinus Nyhoff, 1951.

——, *Estudios sobre Fray Bartolome de Las Casas y sobre la lucha por la justicia en La Conquista Espanola de America*. Caracas, University Central de Venezuela, 1968.

Harpsfield, N. and Roper W., in E.E. Reynolds (ed.), *Lives of Saint Thomas More*. Everyman's Library, 1978.

Hemming, J., *The Conquest of the Incas*. Abacus, 1972.

Henderson, J.S., *The World of the Ancient Maya*. Orbis, 1981.

Irving, W., *Life and Voyages of Columbus*. Tegg, 1866.

Kenny, A., *Thomas More*. Oxford, O.U.P., 1983.

Kristeller, P.O., 'Thomas More as a renaissance humanist', *Moreana*, no. 73, 1980, pp. 5–22.

Kruyfhooft, C., 'The Map of Utopia', *Moreana*, no. 73, 1982, pp. 103–7.

La Garza, M.de, 'Palenque ante de los siglos XVIII y XIX', *Estudios de Cultura Maya*, vol. XIII, 1981, pp. 404–65.

Landa, Fray D. de, *Relaciones de Las Cosas de Yucatan*. Garibay, G.A.M. (ed. and intro.). Mexico, Porrua, 1982.

Las Casas, Fray B. de, 'Opusculos, Cartas y Memoriales', (ed.) Tudelo Bueso, J.P., Madrid, *Biblioteca de autores Espanoles*. vol 110, 1958.

——, *Brevisima Relacion de la destruccion de las Indias*. Madrid, Anjan, 1983.

Lewis, C.S., *English Literature in the Sixteenth Century. Excluding Drama*. Oxford, Clarendon Press, 1954.

Loades, D.M., *Politics and the Nation 1450–1660*. Glasgow, Fontana, 1979.

Lopez Estrada, 'Thomas More en Espana y en La America Hispana', *Moreana*, no. 5, 1965, pp. 27–40.

Lopez de Gomara, F., *Historia General de Las Indias*. 2 vols., Barcelona, Orbis, 1985.

MacKinnon, J.J., 'The Nature of residential Tikal. A spatial analysis', *Estudios de Cultura Maya*, vol. XIII, 1981, pp. 223–49.

Madariaga, S. de, *The Fall of the Spanish American Empire*. London, Hollis and Carter, 1947.

——, 'The Mita and Indian enslavement', in Jensen de Lamar (ed.), *The Expansion of Modern Europe*, pp. 78–82.

Marc'hadour, G., 'Froben et Thomas More en marge de l'edition baloise de l'Utopie', *Moreana*, no. 5, 1965, pp. 113–15.

Martyr, P. de, *Cartas sobre el Nuevo Mundo*. Madrid, Polifemo, 1990.

McConica, J.K., 'The recusant reputation of Thomas More', in Sylvester and Marc'hadour (eds.), *Essential Articles*, pp. 136–49.

Mendelson, E., 'Kermode shoots back' (review of Frank Kermode, *Essays on Fiction*), *The Sunday Times*, 16 Oct. 1983.

Menendez Pidal, R., 'Las Casas and the black legend', in Jensen de Lamar (ed.), *The Expansion of Modern Europe*.

Momprade, E.L. y Gutierrez, T., *Imagen de Mexico, mapas, grabados y litografia*. Mexico, Salvat, 1976.

More, Sir T., *Utopia*. R. Robinson (trans.). Glasgow, Blackie and Sons, 1908.

——, *Utopia*. R. Robinson (trans.), S.J. Lumby (ed.), J.R. C.U.P., 1913.

——, *St. Thomas More. Selected Letters*. E. Rogers (ed.). Yale University Press, 1961.

——, 'Utopia', G. Richards (trans.), in E. Surtz SJ (ed.), *Selected Works of Saint Thomas More*. Yale University Press, 1964.

——, 'Utopia', in E. Surtz SJ and J.M. Hexter (eds.), *Yale Edition of the Complete Works of Saint Thomas More*, vol. 4. New Haven and London, Yale University Press, 1965.

Morison, S.E., *The European Discovery of America. The Southern Voyages 1492–1616*. New York, O.U.P., 1974.

Navarrete, M.F. de, 'Descubrimientos que hicieron por mar los Espanoles: desde fines del siglo XV con varios documentos ineditos', *Viages de Colon, libro 1. Madrid, Emprenta Real, 1825*.

Orosa Diaz, J., *Yucatan, Panorama, Historia, Geografia y Cultural*. Mexico, Biblioteca Enciclopedia Popular 55, 1945.

Parry, J.H., *The Spanish Seaborne Empire*. Hutchinson and Co., 1971.

——, *The Discovery of the Sea*. London, Weidenfield and Nicholson, 1974.

Pena, M. (ed.), *Descubrimiento y Conquista de America, Cronistas, Poetas, Misioneres y Soldades. Una Antologia general*. Mexico, U.N.A.M., 1982.

Popul Vuh. A. Recinos (ed.), Mexico, Fondo de Cultura Economica, 1982.

Prescott, W., *The Conquest of Mexico*. 2 vols, Routledge, 1854.

——, *The Conquest of Peru*. Vol. 1. Philadelphia, 1874.

Prescott, W. and Robertson, W., *The History of the Reign of Charles V with an Account of His Life after His Abdication*. 1869.

Quinn, D.B., 'The argument for the English discovery of America', *Geographical Journal*, vol. CXXVII.

——, 'The English discovery of America', in Jensen de Lamar (ed.), *The Expansion of Modern Europe*. pp. 47–51.

——, *England and the Discovery of America, 1481–1620*. G. Allen & Unwin, 1973.

Rastell, J., *Three Rastell Plays*. R. Axton (ed.). Cambridge, Mass., Braur, Rowman & Littlefield, 1979.

Reynolds, E.E., *Thomas More and Erasmus*. Burns and Oates, 1965.

Rivera Dorado, M., *Los Mayas, Una Sociedad Oriental*. Madrid, Editorial Univ. Complutense, 1982.

Robertson, W., *A History of the Americas*. 1869.

Roukema, E., 'A discovery of Yucatan prior to 1503', *Imago Mundi*, no. XIII, 1956, pp. 30–8.

Ruz Menendez, R., *Ensayos Yucatenses*. Mexico, Univ. de Yucatan, 1976.

Sahagun, Fray B. de, *Historia General de las cosas de Nueva Espana*. G.A.M. Garibay (ed.), Mexico, Porrua, 1982.

Santos g, J., *Los Mayas, y las incognitas del Imperio Antiguo*. Madrid, Paraninfo, 1981.

Scenna, M.A., *Antes de Colon*. Buenos Aires, Univ. de B.A., 1974.

Schoek, R.J., 'Sir Thomas More, Humanist and Lawyer', in Sylvester and Marc'hadour (eds), *Essential Articles*, pp. 569–79.

——, 'More, Sallust and Fortune: Gesner on Utopia's Language', *Moreana*, no. 65, 1980, pp. 107–12.

Scholes, F.V. and Roys, R.L. assisted by Adams, E.B. and Chamberlain, R.S., *The Maya Chontal Indians of Acalan-Tixchel*. Norman. Univ., Oklahoma Press, 1968.

Slavin, A.J., 'Les Langues imaginaire dans le voyage Utopique', *Moreana*, no. 69, 1981, pp. 65–75.

Stapleton, T., *The Life of Sir Thomas More*. Burns and Oates, 1966.

Stephens, J.L., *Incidents of travel in Yucatan*. 2 vols., New York, Dover, 1962.

——, *Incidents of travel in Central America, Chiapas and Yucatan*. 2 vols., New York, Dover, 1969.

Sylvester, R.S., 'Si Hythlodaeus Credimus. Vision and revision in Thomas More's Utopia', in Sylvester and Marc'hadour (eds.) *Essential Articles*, pp. 290–301.

Tapia, A. de., *The Conquistadors*. Cassell, 1964.

Taylor, E.G.R., *Tudor Geography, 1485–1583*. New York, Octagon Books, 1968.

Thompson, J.E.S., *The Rise and Fall of Maya Civilisation*. Victor Gollance, 1956.

Tijeras, E., *Cronica de la Frontera*. Madrid, Jucar, 1974.

Torquemada, Fray J. de, *Monarquia Indiane*, vol. 1., Mexico, U.N.A.M., 1975.

Torres Asensio, J., 'Fuentes Historicas sobre Colon y Americas. Libros rarisimos que saco del olvido.' No. 4, *43 Cartas y lo decado de Pedro Martir Anglieri*, Madrid. 1892.

Trend, J.B., *The Civilisation of Spain*. O.U.P., 1967.

Turner, B.L., 'Agricultura y desarollo del Estado en Las Tierras Bajas Mayas', *Estudios de Cultura Maya*, vol. XIII, 1981, pp. 285–306.

Vaillent, G.C., *The Aztecs of Mexico*. Middlesex, Penguin Books, 1978.

Vespucci, A., *Cartas*. Madrid, Ajana, 1983.

Vila Selma, J., *La Mentalidad Maya*. Madrid, Ed. Nacional, 1981.

Vives, J.L., *60 Lettres de Juan Luis Vives 1492–1540*. A.R. Casanova, (French trans.). Brussels, Valero et Fils, 1943.

Von Hagan, V.W., *Ancient Sun Kingdoms of the Americas*. Paladin, 1973.

Yates, F.A., *Giordano Bruno and the Hermetic Tradition*. Routledge and Kegan Paul, 1971.

Index

Figures in italic refer to numbers of illustrations